Life Lessons From The Hive

M. J. Miller

Jason Barnett, Illustrator

Create Space Publishing

Printed in the United States of America

ISBN-13: 978-1979304023
ISBN-10: 1979304025

DEDICATION

To my two families:
Christ-followers and beekeepers

iii

Praise For

Life Lessons From The Hive

"M. J. Miller takes us safely into the world of the honey bee, a world that is spectacular, magnificent, and direct evidence of an almighty God and His creations."

Keith Elrod, 2014 Tennessee Beekeeper of the year and current President of the Rutherford County Beekeepers Association

"*Life Lessons from the Hive* spoke volumes to me as I read it. M. J. has taken her love for bees and her love for her Heavenly Father and woven them into a beautiful book full of advice, instruction, and encouragement."

Cherie Jobe, Speaker, Life Coach, and Author, *Secrets From Behind the Chair* and *Surviving the Bad Hair Days,* www.cheriejobe.com

"As M. J. Miller interjects the humor of her own personality to explain the life and work of bees, she carries the reader from close understanding of bees to a deeper understanding of life with Jesus. Her parallels not only inform, but they also inspire the reader to contemplate the spiritual purpose of his or her own life."

Twink DeWitt, Author, *The Trust Diamond*

"The way M. J. has compared the body of Christ to the workings of the beehive is brilliant. The perfect order for the beehive is exactly how the body of Christ should operate, everyone doing his part for the ultimate good. The bees' ultimate goal is to care for the queen while a Christian's ultimate goal is to care for the Kingdom. M. J. has hit the nail on the head of this principle. Great whether you are an experienced beekeeper, not a beekeeper at all, or a Christ-follower, this book has something for everyone."

Rev. Jonathan Osterhaus, President, Duck River Beekeepers Association

Contents

Foreword

The Sweetest Thing

In the hills of Tennessee is a place that feels like a little piece of heaven. Bounded by thick woods on one side with fields of clover and a rushing stream on the other, this patch of earth includes a ranch-style home, a lush garden, abundant flowers, and a dozen hives of bees.

Having grown up on a farm, I was used to being around bees. But it wasn't until my wife and I visited the home of our friend and former colleague, M.J. Miller, that I came to recognize how essential bees are to agriculture, our ecosystem and, in fact, our very existence.

Even more amazing to me were how many lessons these tiny, industrious creatures teach us about the nature of God. The Bible abounds with references to honey (62 to be exact). Indeed, the Promised Land was said to be "flowing with milk and honey." But how many of us have ever studied the inside of a hive, where tens of thousands of bees work in harmony to produce the golden nectar we humans (and lots of bears) have prized for centuries?

Only someone with the wisdom, creativity, and observational skills of M.J. Miller could have given us this book. Within her fun and friendly guide to bees, she unlocks secrets of the hive that teach us how to live in harmony with the Creator.

Her stories are as sweet as clover honey on buttered toast. Sit down with a cup of tea or coffee and enjoy this delightful journey into the hive.

Scott Tompkins
Editor, Author, Writing Instructor
University of the Nations

Introduction

Eat honey, my son, for it is good; honey from the comb is sweet to your taste. Know also that wisdom is like honey for you: If you find it, there is a future hope for you, and your hope will not be cut off (Proverbs 24:13-14).

Who knew you could make a connection between bees and God? Well, actually, the well-traveled apostle Paul did. In his letter to the Romans, he said, "For since the creation of the world God's invisible qualities—his eternal power and divine nature—have been clearly seen, being understood from what has been made, so that people are without excuse" (Romans 1:20).

Bees are such little things, yet they are essential to the world's ecology and food supply. While the extent of the damage is debatable, scientists agree that if the honey bee vanished, within three years 70 percent of our food supply would disappear. Imagine a world without apples, oranges, almonds, berries, avocados, onions, vegetables or coffee. We might not starve, but dull dinners would be our daily diet.

When bees work in harmony, they produce honey, the sweetest nectar on earth. So it shouldn't surprise us that God would use bees and honey to teach lessons about His Kingdom.

After almost ten years of doing Christian missions work in Asia and the Pacific with Youth With A Mission (YWAM), God called me back home to a small seven-acre mini-farm in the middle of Tennessee. He paired me up with a fellow missionary, Susan (Suki) Brannan. We had worked together in YWAM and found we made a good team. For over a decade we have used our missions experiences as illustrations in Bible teachings and as international conference speakers.

Not long after we moved to Tennessee, some friends introduced us to honey bees. I was fascinated by these tiny insects, but more than that, I was interested in making honey. While driving the county backroads, I'd often seen hives sitting quietly on the edges of fields, waiting for someone to gather that sweet nectar. How hard could it be?

So, another adventure began with a road trip to a beekeeping supply company in Kentucky with a couple of friends. We were such "newBees," the sales representative had to tell us what equipment we needed. And we bought it all! We looked like the Beverly Hillbillies as we headed back to Tennessee with a truckload of supplies.

Since then I've taken classes in beekeeping, studied and attended many bee conferences, while learning the practical applications from veteran beekeepers. On top of that God taught me even more about the bees by simply sitting with them and observing.

A few years after I began keeping bees, the idea for this book began to hatch in my brain like a baby bee emerging from her cell. Each morning I would take my coffee out to the hives near the house where I sat and watched the bees. As I studied their behavior through the seasons, I came to admire the efficiency of the hive. I also discovered the Lord had more to teach me—not only about the bees but about Himself.

And, little by little, this book was born.

M. J. Miller

"There are certain pursuits which, if not wholly poetic and true, do at least suggest a nobler and finer relation to nature than we know. The keeping of bees, for instance."

Henry David Thoreau

Acknowledgements

As with any major production, there are always more people behind the scenes than on the stage, and that certainly is the case with this book. First, I want to thank Scott and Sandi Tompkins, who nudged me to write a book about bees in the first place, and who kept nudging me throughout the process. They are precious friends and mentors and their contributions, including editing, have been invaluable. I've learned so much from them, I could write a book!

Another treasured friend is my ministry partner, my beekeeping buddy, and my first critic, Susan (Suki) Brannan. I couldn't have finished this project without her. She saw every page long before I dared show it to anyone else and gave me priceless feedback and encouragement. Plus—she loves grammar!

I am also thankful for my many mentors along the way. Three dear friends are at the top of the list: Rev. Dr. Diana M. DeWitt and YWAM leaders Howard and Sue Bruce. They walked with me through many milestones on this faith journey and redirected me when I got off course. Their job wasn't easy, but they hung in there! Their crowns are heavy jewels!

I've never met a beekeeper I didn't like. I'm grateful to the Rutherford County Beekeepers

Association, the Duck River Beekeepers Association, and the Tennessee Beekeepers Association for their excellent instruction. My beekeeping friends taught me more about bees than I ever imagined there was to know. They encouraged me when I needed it and graciously answered all my questions. But with beekeepers, you have to do some sifting, because if you ask 10 beekeepers the same question, you'll get 12 different answers! They love talking about their bees. Heck, they even pray for honey bees!

This project has deepened some friendships and created others. One new friend is my typographer, Nathan R. Sewell. He kept his computer humming into the wee hours of the morning, working with both Jason, my illustrator, and me to format this book and get it ready for publication. Without him, my book would still be taking up file space on my computer.

I've also had life-giving encouragement and help from so many "family and friends." I can't name you all or the Acknowledgments would be longer than the book! I thank God for my support groups, including my church and my Thursday Morning Prayer Group (ENGAGED) who covered this project in prayer—over and over. Our Bible class, the MORE Group, gave me the confidence to begin writing teaching lessons in the first place. And most recently, the Montana Writers Workshop were gentle critics and enthusiastic cheerleaders. Individually and collectively, my friends all lovingly demonstrate the Body of Christ working as it should.

I love you all more than I could ever express—and I'm supposed to be good with words!

Chapter 1 - 60,000 Bees = 1 Hive

"The tools that a society uses to create and maintain itself are as central to human life as a hive is to bee life. Though the hive is not part of any individual bee, it is part of the colony, both shaped by and shaping the lives of its inhabitants."
— Clay Shirky[1]

"Don't be afraid, the bees aren't interested in you." That's what Suki and I tell apprehensive first-time visitors to our bee yard.

After working together in ministry in Youth With A Mission (YWAM) and later as teachers, Suki Brannan and I stepped into the unlikely mission field of beekeeping. Now we incorporate our sometimes funny and sometimes painful experiences from the hives into our Kingdom teachings.

Polls show that 27% of Americans are afraid of spiders and insects (including bees).[2] Bees are fifth on the fear list—behind snakes and public speaking. But if you'll join me, I promise I won't make you recite a speech with a snake in your hand while you stand atop a hive of bees.

2

I want you to be comfortable as we look at and learn from these remarkable insects. I've also included a glossary in the back of the book to help you understand the language of beekeeping. So, why don't you put on your protective veil and come along? After all, there's no better way to get to know bees than to meet them face to face.

One mature beehive houses about 60,000 honey bees. That's a lot of insects with stingers! Beekeepers think of a hive as one unit, like one animal with lots of different moving parts.

Okay. Is your veil on? Good. Let's take a closer look at life inside the hive.

As we carefully lift the wooden lid, we hear the gentle hum of thousands of bees working. The sweet smell of wax and honey, like the embracing aroma of home at Christmas, welcomes us. We lean over to look inside, and hundreds of tiny bee faces pop up between the frames to see who turned on the lights. My smoker, to keep the bees calm, is lit and my hive tool, to pry open the boxes, is in hand.

I puff smoke over the frames and hear the light hum shift to a higher pitch as the bees scurry deeper into the hive. Next, I wedge my hive tool under one of the frames and gently lift it. The frame of honeycomb is covered with bees—over 1,000 of them. They pay no attention to me as they go about the business of feeding brood and storing pollen and honey.

At first glance, all the bees look alike. But there are three types of bees in each hive: drones, workers, and a queen. A healthy hive needs all of these bees working together to survive.

Holding the frame closer, we look for the queen first. There is only one in each hive, and without her, the colony will fail. Measuring about one inch, she's the largest of all the bees, but she's still hard to find. After all, you are looking for a unique bee among thousands—and they just won't stand still!

She's not on that frame, so I carefully replace it and pull another. We spot her hiding under a cluster of bees. Her attendants, who feed and groom her, are trailing behind. The queen's only job is to lay eggs and because she's well cared for she can live five or more years.

Next, we look for the drones. Although there are only a couple hundred of them, they're easy to recognize. Their squarish bodies look like tiny bricks with wings. We can see them wandering around, munching on honey and basically doing nothing. All they do is eat and fertilize the queen. They die in the mating process.

The rest of the bees (all 59,799 of them) are female worker bees. They're the smallest bees in the colony and get their name because they literally do all the work in the hive. They build honeycomb, scout for food and water, gather nectar and pollen, unload and store the "groceries," feed the young eggs and larvae, heat and cool the

4

hive, dehydrate nectar, cap honey, guard the entrance, clean house, take care of the queen and ... take out the trash! These industrious little girls work themselves to death in four to six weeks.

Each bee in the hive has a job to do, and they don't argue about it, unlike some people I know. They work together for the good of the colony. Guard bees sacrifice their lives to defend the hive and foragers die in the field trying to bring in one more load of pollen. God gave the honey bee such a strong sense of community that every bee lives sacrificially for the family.

A community of believers should work that way too. Can we honestly say that we are committed to the body of Christ? Are we willing to die for Jesus or—like Him—lay down our lives for our friends?[3] The answer should be yes, however, sometimes I'd rather my fellow believers lay down their lives for me!

As hard as the idea of dying for Christ is, the harder question seems, "Are we willing to *live* for Him?" It's living for Jesus that challenges us daily. You know what I mean—giving grace to the person who takes advantage of your kindness or the friend who speaks ill of you. It's the day-to-day challenges that are the hardest part of being a Christ-follower.

Let's learn from the bees. They don't jockey for position or seek to overthrow the queen. They simply do what God created them to do—work together to build the hive and produce honey.

As we marvel at the hive's unity, we take one last look before I replace the frame. I point to a baby bee emerging from her cell. We watch as she struggles to pull herself up and out of the opening and begins to stretch. A new life has begun. We both smile—and I believe God smiles too.

Finally, I close the lid. As we turn away from the hives and remove our veils, I see it in your eyes. The bees have charmed you. You're not so afraid of them anymore—and you didn't get stung.

Congratulations!

Do you see yourself as having a purpose to fulfill in the Kingdom of God? How would you describe it?

But in fact, God has placed the parts in the body, every one of them, just as he wanted them to be. If they were all one part, where would the body be? As it is, there are many parts, but one body (1 Corinthians 12:18).

Chapter 2 - A Solid Foundation

For no one can lay any foundation other than the one already laid, which is Jesus Christ (1 Corinthians 3:11).

Here I sit in my garage and makeshift woodworking shop in the cool days of March. I'm repairing old bee boxes and assembling the new equipment I'll need in the spring. The crisp morning air reminds me that winter isn't entirely over, so I have a steaming cup of coffee at hand to stay awake for this tedious task. I wrap my fingers around the warm cup, take a sip and try to think of ways to avoid this job. Why don't I tell you about hive boxes instead?

Wild bees usually live in hollow trees, but if one's not available, they can be pretty creative. Bees have been known to swarm on anything: bicycles, mailboxes, picnic tables, and cars. Beekeepers often get panicked calls to extract these inventive insects from attics, porch columns, behind the walls, in electric boxes or between floors of a house. If there's a hole, the bees will find it.

Obviously, beekeepers prefer to keep bees in hive boxes. The most commonly used hive in North America is the Langstroth hive, named after a honey-loving pastor. In 1852 he got the idea to build a hive box that didn't have to be destroyed each year when collecting honey. Most American beekeepers still use his design today. If you've ever driven in the country, you've probably seen these white sentinels of various heights standing guard at the edges of open fields.

A Langstroth hive body is a precisely measured box with no top or bottom.[4] The boxes can be stacked so the bees can travel freely from one to another. A bottom board for bees to enter and a lid to close the top complete the picture.[5]

The core of the hive is the ten frames in each box: one box—ten frames, two boxes—twenty frames, and so on. You get the picture. Each frame encases a sheet of wax called "Foundation." The bees use the foundation as the backdrop to build or "draw" honeycomb in vertical sheets. Even bees benefit from a good foundation.

Jesus understood the importance of a good foundation. In His first recorded sermon—the Sermon on the Mount—He laid out a foundation for living by challenging His followers to love their enemies. His radical ideas provoked the first century Jews, and they still challenge us today. Try loving the talkative lady telling her life story behind you at the movie or the co-worker whose constant complaining is polishing your last nerve with sandpaper!

At the end of His discourse, Jesus summed up His lesson with an illustration of a house standing through a storm because it was built on a solid foundation.

If you plant a garden, you prepare the soil—foundation; if you knit a sweater, you cast on the right number of stitches—foundation; if you compose a speech or write a paper, you draft an outline—foundation; if you cook a meal, you select the right ingredients—foundation; and, of course, if you build any structure, you build it on a solid foundation. If your foundation is substandard, the finished product could fall apart. The Carpenter would know this.

On His last trip from Caesarea Philippi to Jerusalem, Jesus picks up the foundation theme again. He's talking to Peter about the church and wrapping up His ministry from beginning to end with the same ribbon.

Jesus had asked His disciples the all-important question, "Who do you say I am?" Peter exuberantly proclaimed He was the Messiah. Jesus' response neatly tied that ribbon with a bow and a promise: "... on this rock I will build my church, and the gates of Hades will not overcome it."[6]

The rock, the solid foundation of the church, must be Jesus. If it's not built on Him, when the enemy comes, it will surely crumble as easily as a honeycomb built inside a dead tree.

I was in an earthquake in Hawaii once. I was standing at the entrance of an office talking to the secretary when I felt a distinct shift to the right and then to the left. I'd never been in an earthquake before, and at first, I didn't know what was happening. This was nothing like I'd imagined an earthquake to be. There was no rumble or vibration. Instead, it felt as if someone had taken the building and jerked it from one side to the other.

Books fell over, the ceiling fan swayed, and I grabbed the doorway to keep from falling.

"What was that?" I asked when the movement stopped.

"An earthquake," the secretary replied.

Even though we were shaken and things were scattered around the room, the building stood because it was built on a solid foundation.

If Jesus is the rock on which your life is built, the enemy may shake but he won't overtake you either. There is no more secure place to be.

So sit back and savor your own coffee or tea. I know of a solid rock you can lean on while I get back to assembling these boxes.

Is your hope for the future built on your job, your family or your retirement funds? If so, ask the Lord to help rebuild your foundation.

Therefore everyone who hears these words of mine and puts them into practice is like a wise man who built his house on the rock. The rain came down, the streams rose, and the winds blew and beat against the house; yet it did not fall, because it had its foundation on the rock (Matthew 7:24-25).

Chapter 3 - Ouch!

"I hadn't been out to the hives before, so to start off she gave me a lesson in what she called 'bee yard etiquette.' She reminded me that the world was really one bee yard, and the same rules work fine in both places. Don't be afraid, as no life-loving bee wants to sting you. Still, don't be an idiot; wear long sleeves and pants. Don't swat. Don't even think about swatting. If you feel angry, whistle. Anger agitates while whistling melts a bee's temper. Act like you know what you're doing, even if you don't. Above all, send the bees love. Every little thing wants to be loved." — Sue Monk Kidd, *The Secret Life of Bees*

"Do you ever get stung?" That's the first thing people ask when I say I'm a beekeeper.

My response: "Well, of course, I do." After all, I work with hundreds of thousands of bees.

So, let's talk about stings. I know you've been thinking about it since you opened the book. Right?

In almost everyone's mind, the delicious honey is secondary to the threat of the sting from a tiny bee. Why is that? After all, every job has some risk. If you work with glass, you get cut. If you train dogs, you get bitten. If you swing a hammer, you get your finger smashed. And if you manage bees ...

The good news is most people don't die from honey bee stings. In 2000 the World Health Organization reported only 54 deaths due to bee stings—that's all bees, not only honey bees. More people die from being struck by lightning every year, according to the NOAA Weather Service. And the statistics haven't changed. So, unless you kick over a hive or throw rocks at a swarm, you're probably pretty safe.

On the pain scale listed in the *Atlas Obscura,* the honey bee ranks 17th out of 30 insects.[7] Wasps, hornets and some ants rank higher. However, I don't recommend taking a sampling! Of course, pain levels are subjective (I know my pain is always greater than yours) and varying sensitivity to the toxins cause people to react differently.

Only female honey bees can sting you—that is the workers. The males don't have a stinger, and although the queen does, she won't use it. If a honey bee does sting you, she will die. Her stinger is barbed and when she pulls away, she leaves it and the venom sac behind. In other words, she loses her guts.

The longer the stinger stays in you, the more poison gets under your skin. Obviously, you must remove it, but don't pull the stinger out. Seriously? Grabbing the stinger between your fingers squeezes the venom sac and releases more poison into your body. Instead, use your fingernail or a hive tool to scrape off the stinger.

When people get stung in our apiary, we apply a cooling antihistamine salve. It immediately stops the burning sensation and quickly arrests the pain and swelling. We keep the ointment handy because sooner or later someone gets zapped—and it's usually me.

We all get stung—but not necessarily by bees. Careless words, corrective words, condemning words, corrosive words—they all sting. Some hurt for a short while; others take longer to heal. We toss barbed words around like a mixed salad, not caring where they land.

When I was a kid, we had a retort for stinging words: "Sticks and stones may break my bones, but words will never hurt me!" As an adult, I have a comeback to that nonsense: "Liar, liar, pants on fire!"

We're all allergic to stinging words—but our tolerance levels are different. We wonder why some can endure great pain while others crumble under a thoughtless criticism. The answer is that pain isn't measured in intensity. It's measured in heart damage, which is as real and hurtful as a bee sting.

Have you ever seen a Western where the cowboy was shot with dozens of arrows? That's the picture I get when Scripture calls hurtful words, flaming arrows. All too often we continue to walk around like two-legged porcupines, with needles sticking out everywhere. We need to get rid of those barbs and apply some ointment to our wounds.

The salve that covers heart damage is a blend of forgiveness and love.[8] Both are a choice. While we may want to double down on the darts and return fire, let's choose to reload those arrows with love and send them back in a bow of forgiveness.

Forgiveness is hard. And, frankly, lots of times I don't want to forgive. But if I don't want to get an infection from that stinger, I have to pull it out. I can't ignore it and hope it will go away. Healing can't begin until I scrape off that stinger.

Healing, also, can't be complete until love is applied. Love gives us the ability to bless those who have hurt us—to see them through God's eyes. It comes directly from the throne room of the One who is love.

But how do you know if you've really forgiven someone? Here's the test: Is there anyone you know who, if they walked in the room right now, you'd wish would leave? Take a minute and ask God. If so, forgive them again ... and again until your heart catches up with your words.

That's what Jesus wants us to do. As we return hurt with love, the pain will continue to fade until it's gone.

We've all been stung. Let's not leave the stinger in and pretend it isn't there.

Isn't it time to scrape that thing off and apply some healing salve?

Have you been hurt by stinging words? Are you ready to apply a salve of forgiveness and love?

In addition to all this, take up the shield of faith, with which you can extinguish all the flaming arrows of the evil one (Ephesians 6:16).

Chapter 4 - Pass the Wax

Gracious words are a honeycomb, sweet to the soul and healing to the bones (Proverbs 16:24).

What would you say is a beekeeper's most valuable asset in the hive? If you said honey, you'd be wrong. And, nope, it's not the bees either. It's the honeycomb. Seriously? Even though there are over 20,000 species of bees, only the honey bee makes wax.

As a matter of fact, honey bees are the only species that actually "manufacture" products we can use. Wax has enormous value for humans and bees. We'll look at its value to humans first.

As a personal product beeswax moisturizes skin, clears acne, heals cracked lips, can be used as a salve, a styling gel or mustache cream.

Around the house it can also be used to polish granite or oil furniture joints. If you're working outside it's a handy fix to coat outdoor tools or prevent rust.

We're not done. Throughout history and even today wax has been used to preserve cheese, seal envelopes, waterproof leather and, of course, wax your car. And finally, we all know it's molded and dipped to make candles.

I'm sure there are many more wonderful uses for wax, and as valuable as it is to us, it's even more valuable to the bees. It's the support structure for the whole hive.

Every hive, no matter where it's located—in a box, in a hollow tree or in the walls of your house—has honeycomb. It's where the queen lays her eggs, where the bees raise their young, and where they store their pollen, water, and, of course, their honey.

The wax comes from worker bees that are between 12 and 20 days old. These young girls have working wax glands for only about a week, so if there's comb to be built, they work day and night to get the job done. One bee can produce about eight small waxy scales over a 12-hour period—that's a little over 100 in her lifetime. She converts sugar water to a flaky sheet of wax that's about the size of the head of a pin.

Other bees gather it and chew it to keep it warm and pliable, then pass it on until it is molded into the perfectly measured, interlocking hexagonal honeycomb we recognize.

The hexagon is the strongest design in nature, and it's the most efficient use of space in a crowded hive. Each cell's six precise 120-degree angles create a mathematically efficient architectural design. Who knew bees were mathematicians?

New wax is white so it's easy for a beekeeper to tell when the bees are making wax. It turns yellow with age. Since wax is made from sugar water or nectar, it's only produced by the bees when there's an ample food supply. Bees don't make wax in the dry days of summer or during the cold winter months.

It takes approximately seven pounds of honey to produce one pound of wax. In other words, when the bees have to build comb, not only are they not storing honey, they're eating what reserves they have—seven to one; which is costly for the bees and the beekeeper.

When beekeepers pull a frame from the hive, they can easily spot the bees that are making wax, because they're holding onto one another and hanging off the frame like a chain of monkeys. It's called "festooning." The wax is passed up the chain of bees, like a bucket brigade trying to put out a fire.

Every bee in the wax chain is essential and supports the others. If one bee stops working, the wax won't make it to the comb. Each bee has a responsibility to "pass the wax."

The Scripture from Proverbs that likens gracious words to a honeycomb shows how vital it is for us to affirm and support one another. How can the Kingdom of God advance if we aren't willing to share those words that bring life? In Ephesians 4 Paul says to use our words wisely to build up others according to their needs, so they will benefit.

In a rainy-day world where all we seem to hear is the bad news, wouldn't it be a breath of fresh air to hear some good news for a change?

We're willing to share all sorts of things on Facebook. How about sharing a kind word to someone we meet face to face? We might even see the sun peeking through the clouds a bit if each of us just said one encouraging word to one person each day. But more than encouraging words, let's share the Kingdom.

How would the world know about Jesus if we kept the truth to ourselves? That doesn't necessarily mean we should go to the remote jungles of Africa—although it might. We can share life-giving words wherever we are—in our homes, neighborhoods, at work, school, the ball game or on the golf course.

St. Francis of Assisi suggested we often talk too much when he said, "Preach the Gospel at all times. When necessary; use words." Living and modeling the Kingdom often proclaims the good news without words, and we don't need a theology degree to share a gracious word with those around us. We can simply tell our God stories.

When I say "God stories," I'm not talking about your unedited life-long 4-hour mini-series. That could be like watching the 2000-photo slide show of my summer vacation! I'm talking about simply passing along the little thing (or big thing) God has done for you recently. It can bring some encouragement and open the door wider. If they're hungry for more, then you can plan a time to sit down at a cafe and share your entire testimony.

Like honeycomb in a hive, the Kingdom of God is continually growing, one person at a time. While large numbers usually impress us, Heaven rejoices over every "one" who enters the gates. The gospel was given to each of us by one person doing his part and we also have the opportunity to continue to pass it on. Don't be afraid. Your personal God story is amazing, and there's someone out there who needs to hear it.

So ... pass the wax. There's more comb to be built!

Think of a person in your circle of relationships who needs to hear the gracious words of the Gospel. How might you share the Lord's sweetness with them?

Because we loved you so much, we were delighted to share with you not only the gospel of God but our lives as well (1 Thessalonians 2:8).

Chapter 5 - Who's Calling the Shots?

"Human beings have fabricated the illusion that in the 21st century they have the technological prowess to be independent of nature. Bees underline the reality that we are more, not less, dependent on nature's services in a world of close to 7 billion people"—Achim Steiner, Executive Director UN Environment Programme (UNEP)[9]

Sitting with the bees is dangerous, but not because I might get stung.

Often in the mornings I'll take my coffee to the bee yard and sit with the bees. I like to sip my favorite blend and watch the hive wake up. It's a great way to learn about the bees, and it's a quiet spot to gather my thoughts before the day begins. For me, it's also a special place to meet with God.

This morning, while I watch the bees warming up and stretching as the sun peeks out over the hill, I can't help but consider, who's really in charge here? The hive runs so smoothly and efficiently. Surely, there's a Wax Task Force or a Comb Committee making all the decisions. I know it's not the queen handing out work assignments—she's too busy laying eggs.

For example, the jobs of the workers in the hive are constantly changing. In a matter of days a young worker may graduate from housekeeper to wax maker to nurse bee to queen's attendant to guard bee to forager. Who promotes them? How do they know when to change jobs? How do they graduate to the next position without the other bees getting jealous? I can almost hear their tiny bee voices crying out in frustration, "I want to attend the queen!" "No, it's my turn!"

While they faithfully carry out their tasks in each department, if there's an emergency, every bee stops what she's doing to take care of the crisis. As temperatures drop in winter, the bees cover and insulate the eggs and larvae to protect the young brood. If there's a threat to the hive, they all become guard bees. If the colony is starving, they all starve together. Is this instinct or is something supernatural at work holding everything together?

Did God simply set everything in motion and then let creation direct itself to let the chips fall where they may? Or, if God knows when a sparrow falls,[10] could He also know when a bee dies? And if He knows when a bee dies, is He the One who's really in charge? And if He's the One who's in charge, is He also directing the ants and penguins and flocks of birds flying south for the winter? If that's true, God is really, really, really, really, really big—and busy!

Just look at where my thoughts have gone. I told you sitting with the bees was dangerous!

Scripture tells us that Jesus is the head of the body—that's you and me. But He's not here. He's in Heaven. So, who's really calling the shots?

Most of the time, we are—at least that's what we think as we hopscotch from decision to decision. We're more sophisticated than our ancestors, and we have access to even more information so we turn to technology to sort out our lives. We build houses to keep out the rain, wind, and snow; we package and store food (or buy it) for those mid-afternoon cravings or late-night snacks; and we travel the world faster, farther and with more comfort than ever before. But, let's face it, as sophisticated as we think we are, we're still limited.

We exercise and eat right to stay healthy, yet some extremely fit people die prematurely. We change jobs in order to be more financially secure, yet companies downsize and people lose their livelihood. We put away money for retirement, yet many people become ill and can't enjoy their savings. In Luke 12:16-20, Jesus tells a story about a man who trusted in his wealth instead of God— and his plans fell short too.

When it comes right down to it, we actually control very little in our lives. I didn't choose where or when I would be born, my gender or my parents, the color of my eyes or the shape of my nose. I can't will my heart to beat or keep my hair from turning grey (well, maybe I can do something about my hair).

And when it comes to making decisions, it often looks as if I'm choosing the social flavor of the month. My Big Picture is confined to my finite knowledge, my narrow past experience, and my optimistic, but flawed projection of the future; all of which is limited, at best.

I'm learning the most productive way to run my life is to follow Someone who truly does have the Big Picture. Scripture calls it being led by the Holy Spirit. When we're listening to Him, we're working in unity with the Father, who really does know all things.

Jesus brought us into the family. He modeled a life of following the Holy Spirit, then He commissioned us to "just do it."[11] But how?

By letting the Holy Spirit lead. After all, we're Christ-FOLLOWERS. Why don't we seek His advice when we're faced with a decision? Let's take a minute to listen to His sweet voice before we give an answer. Or maybe we could let Him lead us into a conversation with that stranger standing in the grocery line.

I'm not suggesting we throw up our hands and do nothing. We all have responsibilities and can't skip down the lane of life singing *Que Sera, Sera.* However, when I loosen my grip on the reins a little, I'm more relaxed, and I enjoy the ride more. I've come to realize I'm not really in control anyway, so what do I have to lose? The Holy Spirit may take me through doors I would never have opened on my own—and that's a little scary, but with Him in charge every day becomes an adventure—and a success.

So, why not live dangerously? Grab a cup of coffee, take a moment with God, and invite Him to call the shots in your life.

Who's calling the shots in your life? Are you trying to be the boss or are you being led by the Spirit of God?

For those who are led by the Spirit of God are the children of God (Romans 8:14).

Chapter 6 - The Suit

Therefore put on the full armor of God, so that when the day of evil comes, you may be able to stand your ground, and after you have done everything, to stand (Ephesians 6:13).

Ping! ... Ping! ... Ping!

Bees flew in every direction—angrily buzzing around my head and slamming into my veil as I tried to look into the hive. Bees can smell the carbon dioxide you exhale so when they're on the attack, they go for the face where you're most vulnerable. Their aggression surprised me. It was not going to be a good day—for them or for me.

If you're unprotected, a swarm of angry bees can be dangerous, even deadly. Unless you're allergic to bee stings, it is estimated it takes 1,100 honey bee stings to be fatal,[12] but who wants to volunteer for that case study? Swatting at them only makes them madder and running away isn't always successful. Bees can fly as fast as fifteen miles an hour and while you may be an Olympic Champion, I suspect you'll run out of steam before they do.

No matter how docile a hive may be in the spring, the hot dry months of August and September in Tennessee can cause the bees to become cranky. And I can understand. The bees are crowded; there's almost no nectar to be found; it's hot; there's lots of work to do inside the hive; and to top it all off, the beekeeper has taken the roof off the house, turned on the light, and rearranged the furniture!

So there I stood, hive tool in one hand and a smoker in the other trying to peer through 60,000 bees to see what was causing this frenzy. It's unnerving, to say the least, when you look like the Peanuts character, Pigpen, but instead of dust, you're covered in bees! I was grateful I had on my bee suit.

Every beekeeper wears some protection when opening a hive—it's Beekeeping 101: Don't go into a hive without a smoker, a hive tool, and a bee suit. The smoker is used to cover up the bees' ability to smell and interrupts their communications with one another. The hive tool, a chisel-like bar, helps pry apart the boxes and the suit is your protection against bee stings.

A bee suit is a one-piece white zippered coverall with elastic at the wrists and ankles. The hat and veil are zipped to the jacket to protect your head and face. With the addition of gloves and shoes there's no way for the bees to crawl inside and make you sorry you ever became a beekeeper. Even people who can't dance have learned a step or two when an angry bee has buzzed up a loose pant leg!

So, when I go out to work the bees, I'm intentional. It's their nature to defend their home, so I don't waste time. I know what I'm looking for and what I'm planning to do. I move slowly and carefully because I know what it's like to be stung. And while one or two stings isn't bad, I don't want to be unprotected when thousands of those little girls get a "bee in their bonnet!"

As Christ-followers, we know we face opposition. We have an enemy who is looking for any small opening he can find. If we're not protected, he'll quietly crawl in and work unnoticed until we feel the sting.

Our enemy will do as much damage as he can, within the boundaries God has set. There are rules of engagement. Just as a single bee can't sting you more than once, the enemy is limited to the damage he's allowed to inflict. He can only enter through an open door, and he can only stay as long as you let him. Once you command him to leave, he must go.

Paul reminds us that our struggle is not against people, but against the spiritual forces influencing those people. So we need God's wisdom to know how to engage in the battle.

We don't need a quicker wit or a sharper tongue. We require kneepads. That's right. We fight the enemy with prayer. Prayer shifts the atmosphere by turning up the heat on the enemy.

When we pray, we invite the forces of Heaven to take the field on our behalf.

While we're in the midst of this spiritual battle, though, we can have complete confidence because God has equipped us totally. Not only do we have weapons of offense, but we also have a strong defense. We are totally protected.

In Ephesians 6 Paul says, "Put on the armor of God," and he describes a Roman suit of armor—the best protection a soldier could have in his day. Paul is reminding us that we are all called to war, but we can be confident we're protected.

Christ-followers don't need smokers and hive tools; they need truth, faith, righteousness, the Word of the Lord, the power of the Holy Spirit, and a readiness to step into battle. We're in a war whether we like it or not, so we might as well come suited up and with a plan. After all, we have the assurance that the battle is already won.

That's right. The enemy is already defeated, even though he doesn't know it yet—like a limb cut from a tree—it may still be green, but it's already dead. So Satan goes on the offensive, like the bees—Ping! ... Ping! ... Ping! You have to stand up to him, know your authority, and use it. If you do, he'll be sorry you got out of bed this morning. Remember. Before you go into battle ...

Zip up your suit.

Are you ready for battle? Are there any pieces of your armor that need mending?

Finally, be strong in the Lord and in his mighty power. Put on the full armor of God, so that you can take your stand against the devil's schemes. For our struggle is not against flesh and blood, but against the rulers, against the authorities, against the powers of this dark world and against the spiritual forces of evil in the heavenly realms (Ephesians 6:10-11).

Chapter 7 - Tools of the Trade

For the word of God is alive and active. Sharper than any double-edged sword, it penetrates even to dividing soul and spirit, joints and marrow; it judges the thoughts and attitudes of the heart (Hebrews 4:12).

"I saw your hives from the road, and I wanted to talk to you about your bees." The stranger in my driveway introduced himself. He was a new neighbor.

My ears perked up. Beekeepers love talking about their girls.

"Do you have bees?" I asked.

"No," he shifted his weight. "I found a swarm in my yard today and thought I would catch them and start a hive ... "

"That's great," I replied.

"So, ... I thought I might be able to buy some used boxes from you."

"Okay ... " I hesitated as I looked around my garage cluttered with bee equipment.

"My daddy used to keep bees when I was a kid," he continued, "and I thought I might give it a try."

"Do you have a bee suit or a smoker or hive tool?" I asked, mentally calculating how many extra boxes I had.

"Well, no," he answered.

I turned and looked at him. "Then you probably shouldn't try to keep this swarm."

He seemed disappointed so I explained. "You don't have the essentials. Beekeeping is more than having a box of bees in your yard. You have to have the right tools so you can manage them responsibly. Otherwise the bees will suffer—and so will you."

"Besides a suit, you'll need this," I said as I reached into my supply wagon and pulled out my smoker. "When you open the hive, guard bees send out a distress signal with their scent glands, like a tsunami or tornado siren. Smoke masks the alarm pheromone so the bees remain calm," I concluded.

As my new friend examined the smoker, I reached back into the wagon and grabbed a hive tool. "You'll also need one of these." I handed him a 12-inch-long flat steel bar with a hook on one end and a beveled edge on the other. "The bees glue everything together, including the boxes, so you'll need a hive tool to pry them apart. It's almost impossible to separate boxes and pull out frames without one."

Many believers are like my neighbor. We call ourselves Christ-followers, but some of us don't have the essential tools. Others have the tools, but don't use them. Let me reach into my believer's supply wagon and show you.

The Bible is the first tool we need. God calls it the Sword of the Spirit. Scripture is God's love letter to us, His guidebook and His owner's manual. Its pages reveal who God is, what He wants to say to us, and how we can successfully navigate our way through life's bumpy terrain. We should read the Bible regularly and apply its truth to our lives. The Bible is the most important book you'll ever own.

Prayer is another essential tool. It is so vital to our Christian walk that Jesus gave us a model: the Lord's Prayer.

While there are many "types" of prayers (intercession, petitions, repentance and praise, to name a few), basically prayer is talking to God. And sometimes it's quietly sitting in His Presence.

Former CBS anchor Dan Rather found himself unprepared for a television interview with Mother Teresa more than 20 years ago. "When you pray," asked Rather, "what do you say to God?"
"I don't say anything," she replied. "I listen."
Rather tried another tack, "Well, okay...when God speaks to you, then, what does He say?"
"He doesn't say anything. He listens."
Rather looked bewildered. For an instant, he didn't know what to say.

"And, if you don't understand that," Mother Teresa added, "I can't explain it to you."[13]

Personally, I love simply sitting with Him—it's my favorite way to pray. I like to begin the day in quiet God-dialogues and when I invite Him to join me, He always shows up. How can we get to know someone if we never talk to them?

Another tool Christ-followers need is fellowship. Bible teacher Dean Sherman, says, "Nowhere in the Bible does it say you can be a Christian by yourself." Jesus established a community of believers with His disciples; Peter and James continued the fellowship in Jerusalem; and Paul founded churches throughout the Mediterranean. Connecting to a biblically strong community keeps us grounded in God's truth, holds us accountable, and provides support when we're fragile.

If your walk with God is more like plodding on a treadmill than strolling down a path, why don't you try one of these tools? The right tools really do make a difference.

My neighbor didn't get the swarm that day. I did. But when he does get the essential tools, I'll be happy to help him learn to work with the bees.

Because like Christ-followers, new beekeepers need mentors, too.

Are you using the tools God has given you? How could you make better use of them?

All Scripture is God-breathed and is useful for teaching, rebuking, correcting and training in righteousness (2 Timothy 3:16).

Chapter 8 - You Are What You Eat

But you are a chosen people, a royal priesthood, a holy nation, God's special possession, that you may declare the praises of him who called you out of darkness into his wonderful light (1 Peter 2:9).

"Eat your peas," my mom would say while I stubbornly sat at the table, my lips pursed and my arms crossed.

"No."

"They're good for you."

"I don't care." (To clarify, I was five. I don't act like that at the dinner table today.)

I think every child growing up goes through similar dinner disputes. Very few of us kids were like Mikey, who would eat anything.[14] Our palettes mature with age and, hopefully, our manners do too. But, as I've grown older—and somewhat wiser—I now agree with my mother—and my doctor: What you eat does make a difference.

The queen bee is a perfect example. She is about twice the size of a worker bee with a shiny sleek thorax. Her wings, which are the same size as a worker's, look short against her long elegant

44

body. She isn't covered with fuzzy hairs like other bees and often she's a solid color with little or no stripes. So what makes her so different? Is she a separate species? The simple answer is "No." The complex answer is below.

A queen begins her life like every other female bee—as an egg. And, like all eggs, she is fed royal jelly, a nutrient-rich food, for the first three days of her life. Day three is when the bees make a distinction between this queen-to-be and the rest of the girls. That's when every other egg's diet shifts to a mixture of pollen and honey, but the future queen continues to be fed nothing but royal jelly. What she eats not only changes her looks, it changes her anatomy.

By eating royal jelly she grows larger than the other females. Even as a larva she is bigger, so the bees create a special cell for her. This oversized pitted cell, looking like a peanut, is usually easy to spot on a frame of evenly capped brood. Beekeepers cleverly named this peanut a "queen cell."

When the queen larva is five and a half days old, the bees seal her up in her "Princess Peanut" where she will continue to eat stored royal jelly. After 16 days she will step on to the stage—a fresh young monarch. It's the royal jelly—and that alone—that sets her apart. Because of her diet she now has the capacity to mate and store fertilized eggs as long as she lives—something other female bees can't do. She is different inside and out and her diet of royal jelly will continue for the rest of her life.

Like the queen bee, what we eat affects how we look too. Our bodies need proper nourishment to thrive and so do our spirits. We were born with lots of natural appetites, but they aren't all good for us. There's a reason some food is called "junk food." Let's learn to choose which appetite we will feed.

What we gobble up at the dinner table affects how we function. If we don't eat enough healthy food, we'll be lethargic and weak. An overdose of sugar or caffeine and we're bouncing off the walls; mounds of chocolate or ice cream can make us fat and sluggish; and too many vegetables can ... well, you get the point.

Besides eating good food, we also need to eat regularly. One meal, no matter how delicious or filling, will not sustain us throughout our entire life. Take Thanksgiving. We gorge ourselves on plates piled high with juicy turkey blanketed by homemade dressing and gravy with all the fixings until we're as stuffed as the turkey! Then, we top it off with dessert.

We congratulate the cook while lamenting the fact that our eyes are bigger than our stomachs. Then we push back from the table for some exercise in the form of loosening our belts and waddling to the recliner to watch other people play football. And after an energizing two-hour nap, we're back in the kitchen munching on another piece of pumpkin pie!

God designed our bodies to require regular nourishment to survive. So it should be no surprise our spirits need regular feeding too. One hour in church on the weekend will barely give me enough "fuel" to exit the parking lot without losing my Christianity as I race my fellow believers to the local restaurant for lunch.

If we fill our lives with the things of the world, we will grow to look like the world. But if we fill up on the things of God, we will become more like Him.[15] What we watch, what we listen to, and what we dwell on are the things that feed our spirits. Perhaps we can turn off the TV and turn on the praise music. Close our computers and open our Bibles. It makes a difference.

What we feed will grow and what we starve will die. Sometimes, we have to stop feeding our old nature. We simply have to learn to say, "No," to ourselves. The Bible calls that self-control. In Galatians, Paul says it's a fruit of the Spirit.

As we begin to starve ourselves of the things that dull our senses, we'll find we have a new appetite for things which ignite our spirits. Maybe it's time to remove some items from our pantry and restock our spiritual shelves with healthy food.

As Christ-followers, our first priority is to feed ourselves regularly with good food.[16] So let's skip the appetizers and get into the meat of the Bible. It's a good place to start. Ask the Holy Spirit to give you revelation as you read God's Word. You'll be delighted with the savory meal that's in store.[17]

So what are you waiting for? Open up that jar of royal jelly, and let's eat!

What appetites are you feeding? Do you need to change your diet?

But solid food is for the mature, who by constant use have trained themselves to distinguish good from evil (Hebrews 5:14).

Chapter 9 - Did Someone Call for a Nurse?

I gave you milk, not solid food, for you were not yet ready for it. Indeed, you are still not ready (1 Corinthians 3:2).

I never liked math in school. I barely made it through the minimum requirements, and I've long since forgotten almost every formula I ever memorized. Heck, if I add or subtract anything over ten I have to take off my shoes so I can use my toes! So you can imagine my apprehension when I found out that understanding the numbers is an important part of beekeeping.

The queen is the royal mother of every bee in the hive and in the spring and summer, a good queen will lay an average of one egg every 30 to 60 seconds. That's about 1,500 eggs a day. (And you thought you had a houseful of kids!) This monarch is an extraordinary egg-laying machine, but she's a terrible mother. Her sole job in the hive is to make sons and daughters. She walks across the comb inspecting cells to make sure they're clean and polished, and when one meets her approval, she lays an egg in it and then moves on, leaving those baby bees to be cared for by others.

50

What's a mother to do? She doesn't have time to bond with all those 1,500 children. So she depends on other bees to tend to the kids. Those pint-sized caregivers are called "Nurse Bees." That's right, I said, "Nurse Bees."

For those of you who like numbers, here we go. It's estimated that 110,000 feeding visits are made to a single bee during the nine days it's in the egg and larval stage. That means each egg and baby bee is fed over 12,000 times a day. Multiply that by the 1,500 eggs the queen lays in one day and that comes to 18,000,000 feedings a day! Let me write it out—eighteen MILLION. That's a lot of formula! Plus, (notice my mathematics term) every 24 hours another 1,500 eggs are added to the baby bee basket, increasing the feedings by another 18 million daily, and so on. Multiply that by the nine-day cycle, and it equals 162 million feedings. Obviously, the phrase "Busy as a bee!" is an understatement!

Caring for all those young bees is an enormous investment of time and resources from the hive. As a matter of fact, from the bees' perspective, that's the whole purpose: raising bees.

Those baby bees, who consume half their body weight a day, are carefully looked after by young Nurse Bees who, only a few days ago, were baby larvae themselves. These little insects will do everything they can to care for and protect their young. They know that newly born sons and daughters can't be left on their own. They need nurturing.

The Kingdom of God should be growing in the same way. God calls us sons and daughters—spiritual sons and daughters.[18] When we become Christ-followers, we don't join a club; we're born into a family. The family design was so strong in the heart of God, He used it as a template throughout all of creation—beginning with Adam and extending even down to the honey bee.

God loves the family. That's why the devil wants to destroy it. Our enemy knows that family is one of the most powerful influences in our lives. As children we all want someone to be proud of us. As adults, we recognize how fragile little hearts can be.

As a body of believers, we don't need more programs, we need more parents. We can't be satisfied with only salvations, and we can't leave the job of parenting to the person behind the pulpit.

We all need faith-filled mothers and fathers—pastors, leaders, and spiritually mature friends—who feed us, teach us and mentor us as we navigate around the potholes of life.

Have you ever eaten great barbecue cooked in a microwave? Probably not. Master grillers know "slow" is the key to a tender brisket or melt-in-your-mouth ribs. They smoke their meat at low temperatures for hours or even days so it's fork-tender and juicy. Good investments have the long view in mind. Good mentors do, too.

Our world is filled with hurting and broken people who are looking for real answers; not whimsical distractions, express discipleship or plastic piety. We need honest relationships with people who care enough to speak truth; not 500 Facebook friends who give a thumbs up to our random musings or photos of our exquisite dinner (which probably was not cooked in a microwave).

Just as bees are intentional about caring for their young, the church also needs to be intentional about raising strong Christ-followers. There's much more to this Kingdom life than salvation. Both Paul and the writer of Hebrews addressed this problem in the church centuries ago, and it's still an issue today.[19] There will always be new believers who need milk; but there are many more of us *mature believers* who haven't yet modified our diet from milk to solid food.

I'm told the Dead Sea is dead because it has no outlet. The minerals are so concentrated that nothing can live in it because water comes in but it never leaves. Christianity isn't about being consumers. We should be springs of living water, not stagnant pools. As others have invested in us, it's time for us to "pay it forward."

So go ahead and drink those 18 million glasses of milk if you need to. But when you're finished, put on your nursing hat, and start pouring for someone else.

Are you investing in others? If not, how can you begin?

The third time (Jesus) said to him, "Simon, son of John, do you love me?" Peter was hurt because Jesus asked him the third time, "Do you love me?" He said, "Lord, you know all things; you know that I love you." Jesus said, "Feed my sheep," (John 21:17).

Chapter 10 - Flying Solo

"Aerodynamically, the bumblebee shouldn't be able to fly, but the bumble bee doesn't know it so it goes on flying anyway." — Mary Kay Ash

Have you ever flown around the world— three times? In six weeks, a hive of bees will fly 90,000 miles, three global orbits, to collect a little over two pounds of honey. Talk about jet-lag— especially when you remember a worker bee only lives six weeks!

Generally, the first 14-21 days of a bee's life are spent in the hive. It's not until the last three weeks of her life that she leaves the hive to forage for food and water. In her final 21 days she will travel about 500 miles.

A bee's wing stroke is about 200 beats per second, which is why she has that distinctive buzzing sound. She doesn't flap her wings up and down like a bird, her flutter is from side to side, like a mini-helicopter. That's why she can do what seems impossible—fly. Besides, she never read the books that said she couldn't.

When a bee gathers food, she visits between 50 and 100 flowers on each collection flight.

Entomologists (folks who study insects) have reported that forager bees can make more than 100 foraging trips a day, which adds up to more than 5000 flowers each day—for one bee!

A forager focuses on the task of gathering food. She leaves the safety of the hive, battling the weather and avoiding dragonflies and birds while she moves from flower to flower sucking up nectar and gathering pollen. She stores the nectar in a special honey stomach, where she adds the enzymes necessary to turn the nectar into honey. If she's gathering pollen, she packs it in pockets on her hind legs.

Forager bees are the oldest bees in the hive, and if you happen to see one in your garden, you might notice that her wings are tattered and torn. This is the last season in her delicate life, and she's flying solo.

This lone honey bee flits from flower to flower gathering groceries, but she's not toiling for herself, she's working for the colony. She can't survive alone, so like a homesick child, she always returns home for the night.

The power of community is what keeps a colony alive. Even if they run out of food, they will all starve as a group, sharing the last drop of honey evenly. It's togetherness to the max.

So why do we think we can be "lone rangers" when it comes to our own lives? We say we're tough and don't need anybody, but that's not true. Untouched babies don't thrive. Isolated young people often become depressed and socially crippled. And abandoned seniors are overtaken by their old age.

God understands the power of community in bees and in humans. That's why He created families and why He places us in churches. We need the fellowship of other believers. And the people we hang out with have an influence on us. So it makes sense that we should surround ourselves with folks who will encourage us and point us to Jesus. It's unrealistic to believe we can grow to spiritual maturity on our own.

It saddens me when I hear someone say they don't need a church—their relationship with God is "personal." Of course, our relationship with God should be personal, but it's not private. If we truly have a friendship with the Lord, we can't hide it.[20] It affects how we work, how we play, how we do business, and how we relate to our friends and family. Jesus should be leaking out of us and splashing on everything we do and everyone we meet.

Remember Moses? God called him up to Mount Sinai for intimacy, and after forty days with the Lord, Moses' face glowed! That's intense fellowship. Yet God wouldn't let him stay there. He sent Moses back down to be with the people—three times![21]

Isolation is a tactic of the enemy. He wants to get you alone so you can't hear any voice but his. Satan's voice gets louder while the still small voice of God gets lost in the clutter. The fellowship of believers can bring truth into your life, shine a light on the hazards ahead, and keep you from running aground. When we don't have a solid community around us, it's easy to gradually slip into error.

Like forager bees gathering nectar, missionaries who are alone in the field often don't survive. Not because they can't handle the difficulties, but because they don't have the support system to keep them on track, to pray for them and to encourage them.

Missionaries need a team, and Christ-followers do too. We all need our own personal group of cheerleaders, whether it's a small group, a Sunday school class, a prayer group or a Christian club. Those are the folks who will pray with and for us when we're down, who will celebrate with us over the victories, and who will love us enough to tell us when we miss the mark.

We've all heard the phrase, "There's safety in numbers." Well, it's true. When Jesus sent His disciples out to minister, He sent them two-by-two. When God called Suki and me out of YWAM and into the hills of Tennessee, He called us to go out together also. Not only do we minister together, but we also hold each other accountable. Being part of a team is a Kingdom principle.

Don't allow yourself to become isolated.

You're an easy target for the enemy when you fly solo.

Have you ever tried flying solo when you really needed help from others? What are some things you can do to keep from becoming isolated?

We proclaim to you what we have seen and heard, so that you also may have fellowship with us. And our fellowship is with the Father and with his Son, Jesus Christ (1 John 1:3).

Chapter 11 - The Great Escape

He said to them, "Go into all the world and preach the gospel to all creation" (Mark 16:15).

Suki and I heard an amplified buzzing in the apiary the other day. Yep, there they were—thousands of frenzied bees zipping through the air—SWARM! And I was standing right in the middle of them! It's unnerving. The sound alone is enough to make a smart person run for cover. Not me. Does that say something about my survival instinct or my intelligence?

I stood still and watched this fascinating event in the life of a hive. Bees were swirling around my head, but I didn't move. I wanted to see where they would settle. My first thought was, *Hopefully, I can catch it.*

I watched as the great horde of bees gradually began to recalibrate. The mass of bees got smaller and smaller as they zeroed in on their target—the branch of a nearby tree. Obviously, the queen had landed there and the rest of the bees were honing in on her pheromone.

In about fifteen minutes, all 5,000 or so bees had settled in a tight cantaloupe-sized cluster around her majesty. The small swarm wouldn't survive the coming winter, but it was large enough to become a healthy colony with some help, so Suki and I decided to catch it.

Suki held the ladder while I climbed up and carefully cut the small 10-inch branch where they had gathered. I gently placed it in a new hive box. Done! The next day I would remove the branch and replace it with frames of foundation so the bees could settle into their new home.

The idea of catching a swarm is intimidating to a first-time beekeeper, but it's really pretty simple. The primary concern for the beekeeper is to capture the queen. Usually, if you have her, the rest of the bees will follow. But each swarm is different, and some are easier to get to than others. In this case, we simply had to clip a small limb from the tree.

When a hive gets too crowded, it will swarm. The bees just buzz off!

Swarms usually occur in the early spring when the colony builds up quickly. After all, the queen is laying over 1,500 eggs a day, increasing the number of bees in each colony by over 10,000 a week. That's serious multiplication—and overcrowding!

Swarming is the bees' way of keeping the hive alive. If they think they're too crowded or the queen's not performing well, the bees will begin raising a new princess. Before the new queen is about to hatch, the old monarch and about half of the bees in the hive will leave. That's called a swarm. The swarm can be as small as a few hundred bees, about the size of a baseball, or it can have tens of thousands of bees in it as big a beachball.

Before the bees leave home, they start packing for the trip by gorging on honey. Then when everyone's ready, the swarm of mostly younger bees with the old queen come boiling out of the hive's entrance. They look for a convenient spot nearby where they can settle temporarily while scouting out a new home.[22] A few bees visit several locations while the rest of the swarm clusters around the queen. Once they decide on where to build a house, they will move. When they arrive in their new digs, they quickly begin to make comb so the queen can continue to lay eggs, the next generation of bees.

In human terms, swarming takes a great deal of courage. Most of these young bees are less than three weeks old and have never left the hive. The queen also is in unfamiliar territory. She has never been outside except for the few days when she took her mating flights. None of these bees has ever swarmed before, and there's no one to teach them how. They simply "step out in faith." Get it?

Sometimes God asks us to step out of our comfort zone, too. Like the bees, it's a way of multiplying the Kingdom, but it may be scary. Every so often God asks us to do something we've never done before, in a place we've never been, and with no one to show us how. I don't know about you, but I get uncomfortable when I think about moving into new territory. I'd much rather be home curled up on the sofa reading a good book about the Kingdom of God.

But God loves to challenge us. And one day, for many of us, a season will come when the Lord says, "It's time." Time to take that class. Time to speak to that neighbor. Time to go on that mission trip. Frankly, I think God likes to mix things up a bit—you know, keep us off balance. Consequently, we have to rely on Him to prevent us from tipping over.

That means we have to stop simply reading about the Kingdom and start actually exploring the possibilities out there.

In 2015, there were 2.3 billion Christians in the world (32 percent of the population).[23] Can you imagine the effect we would have on the world if half of us stepped out in faith and brought one person into the family?

It's a little like swarming. Think of how many new colonies we could start. Talk about a revival!

Jesus tells us to go out into the world. He doesn't tell the world to come to us. Generally speaking, the world isn't going to come knocking on your door. That's not how walking by faith works.

Maybe it's time to put down that book about the Kingdom, pack our bags with the "honey" of the Holy Spirit—and swarm.

What's God nudging you to do?

Truly I tell you, Jesus replied, no one who has left home or brothers or sisters or mother or father or children or fields for me and the gospel will fail to receive a hundred times as much in this present age: homes, brothers, sisters, mothers, children and fields—along with persecutions—and in the age to come eternal life" (Mark 10:29-30).

Chapter 12 - Do You Wanna Dance?

David was dancing before the LORD with all his might (2 Samuel 16:4).

"What in the world ... ?"

That was my reaction the first time I saw a bee do the well-documented and often studied "waggle dance." Looking at the frame of bees, I saw one bee walking around in a loose figure-eight pattern, vibrating like someone had stuck her antenna into an electrical outlet. These distinctive gyrations stood out among the relatively calm bees going about the everyday business of maintaining the hive. But why dance? What was going on?

Bees have an extremely small brain, so scientists question how they even came up with the dance in the first place, why they do it, and how they interpret it. Careful study has shed some light on the "what" and "why." While we use language and landmarks to give directions, the twirling and vibrating dance of a forager bee tells the other bees where to find a good source of nectar or pollen. As for the "how," Barbara Shipman, an expert in multi-dimensional mathematics at the University of Rochester whose father was a beekeeper, speculates that the waggle dance is possibly a projection of a shape from the 6th dimension.[24]

The alignment of the figure-eight pattern of the dance points to the direction of the flower source. The duration of the gyrations and width of the pattern also indicate how far away the flowers are—all triangulated in relation to the hive, the flowers and the sun. Other bees need this information because when they forage, they only consume enough honey to take them to the flowers and back. They can't afford to run out of gas on the way home so they pay close attention to this gyrating girl.[25]

This whirling bee dances with all her might for about 30 minutes sharing the good news of her find with her sisters. Basically, she's saying, "Hey, Girls! There's a great spot of clover about 200 yards away and fifteen degrees west of the sun."

Interestingly, this little foot-stomping bee twirls on the dance floor of the comb in the darkness of a closed hive. So how does this pirouetting performer tell the rest of the bees where the flowers are if they can't see the dance? Actually, they "feel the music" by picking up the signal through vibrations on the comb.

Like a flying seismograph, every part of a bee's body is covered with tiny hairs—super-sensitive feelers recording every vibration. So when a bee twirls over the comb, it feels like an earthquake to the rest of the hive.

But there's a problem. In the 30 minutes it takes to perform the waggle dance, the sun has moved! *Uh oh!*

Not to worry. While a bee's brain is only the size of a sesame seed, she can calculate the distance and direction to a flower source faster than a computer! (It's that sixth dimension mathematics thing.) The bees adjust their flight path like an air traffic controller. Once they get close to the flowers, their incredible sense of smell takes over so they can take advantage of this precious patch of paradise—all because of one dancing bee.

David was a dancer, too. He danced when he brought the ark of the covenant into Jerusalem.[26] Even though he was king of Israel, he took off his royal robes and danced with abandon as the ark came through the city gates. He didn't care what anyone thought of him. God had changed his life, and he wasn't the least bit shy when it came to showing everyone how much he loved his God.

How about us? Are we too stuffy or embarrassed to "dance?" Does our dignity outweigh our desperation? Coming into a personal relationship with Jesus is as earth-shattering as two tectonic plates colliding. It rocks and wrecks our world. It's an event worth celebrating, yet we often hide it from others. We're afraid someone may be offended by our Jesus so we zip our lips and hold our tongue.

Scripture says the fear of man is a trap that leaves us bending in whatever direction the wind blows. We all want to be accepted, and while we may say, "I love God above all else," peer pressure says don't rock the boat. So we sit still trying not to move in order to blend in with the crowd. Not David.[27]

His love for God was so overwhelming that he wrote and sang over one hundred songs about it. He was not embarrassed about his relationship with God, and God rewarded him. He called David a man after His own heart and then He did something amazing. He established David's throne forever. How?

Jesus was a direct descendant of David, and when Jesus (of the family line of David) takes the throne, it will be forever.

What the world calls foolishness, God calls passion. I don't know about you, but I want to be known by God as one who is passionate about Him. And even though I'm a bit embarrassed to dance before the Lord even when I'm alone, I'm working on it. And God doesn't mind if I miss a step or two.

Isn't it time we lay down our inhibitions and start dancing? Our salvation is worth celebrating so let's put on our party hats, light up the mirror ball, and step on to the dance floor. We don't have to lead the whole hive to the flowers, all we have to do is dance where we are. The little vibration we start may be an earthquake in someone else's life.

If we're willing to dance, God will stimulate the antennae of others with the wafting of His sweet fragrance so they, too, can zero in on the Promised Land.

Are you willing to dance before the Lord no matter what people say? What does that look like to you?

Fear of man will prove to be a snare, but whoever trusts in the LORD is kept safe (Proverbs 29:25).

Chapter 13 - The Mighty Mite

"The only reason for making a buzzing noise that I know of is because you are ... a bee! The only reason for being a bee that I know of is making honey ... and the only reason for making honey is so I can eat it." — Winnie the Pooh in A. A. Milne's *The House at Pooh Corner*

"Let's play!"

A brightly colored beach ball slammed into my head throwing sand in my face. *There goes my quiet day relaxing by the sea.* Yep, I'm on vacation taking in a few rays at the beach, but I'm still thinking about bees. That's the problem with beekeepers—whether you're in the mountains or at the beach, you're never far from your hives—at least in your heart.

Beach Balls. I threw this one back and the kids headed further down the beach. I dusted off my magazine and resumed reading the article about bee pests. (Only beekeepers read articles about bees at the beach!) *Where was I? Oh, yes. Pests.*

Like Winnie the Pooh, bears do like honey and they're natural enemies of the bees which is

74

why beekeepers don't wear black. Bears can literally turn a bee's world upside down in a matter of minutes. But bears aren't the bees' only enemy. There's a smaller pest that can do much more permanent damage to a hive. It's called the varroa mite.

Under a microscope a varroa mite looks like a small tick—a bee tick. It's a parasite that attaches itself to adult bees and larvae and literally sucks the life out of them. Proportionately to a human, a mite on a bee would be about the size of a beach ball stuck to your neck. These insects hitch a ride into the hive on the backs of adult bees. And, while the bee might be able to remove some of the mites, if she leaves even one, she's doomed to carry this killer with her, infecting everything she does until it completely destroys her.

Varroa mites also attack defenseless baby bees. These leeches hop off the adults while they feed the larvae, moving into the baby bees' cells. When bees cap the cells, the mites are sealed inside where they attach themselves to the young and lay their own eggs. By the time the young bee emerges from her cell she may have three or four mites stuck to her, and she will be in such a weakened state she will soon die. Then the mites on her will simply move on to another host bee and continue the cycle, growing and feeding on even more larvae.

If this cycle is left unchecked, the whole hive will eventually die. As the bees become weaker, other diseases develop until the hive is destroyed. It's an ugly scenario, and here's the cruel truth— every hive has at least some varroa mites! They aren't easily seen, but they're there.

What's a beekeeper to do?

One solution is to break the mite's breeding cycle. If the queen stops laying for several weeks, the mites have no larvae to feed on and will starve or leave. So, you may ask, why would a queen stop laying? Swarming! When a hive swarms, there's about a three-week period when there are no new larvae in the hive, which keeps the varroa population to a minimum.

Hmm ... Break the cycle and stay clean. Have you figured out where this one's going?

Sin is crouching at the door, just waiting to devour us. It may be small at first, like a mite, but it will spread if we ignore it. The enemy is crafty and subtle. He uses his tailor-made weapon, the lie, to get a foot in the door with convincing comments like "That won't hurt you." "Everyone does it."

If we continue to carry Satan's lies through life, sin will infiltrate every thought and life situation until, like the varroa mite, it has contaminated everything we touch and everyone we care for. If we don't deal with sin, it will destroy us.[28]

You see, God doesn't call things "sin" because He wants to spoil our fun. He didn't create an arbitrary list of dos and don'ts to see who will cross the line. His plan for us is abundant life, and sin causes us to miss the mark. He knows that sin will ultimately bring us death.

Getting rid of sin is the first step. But sometimes we get caught in a loop of sinning, repenting, sinning again and repenting again. Over and over. That's when we have to break this cycle in our lives, change our way of thinking, and begin moving in the opposite direction.

That course correction may mean changing our habits or making new friends. We might have to stop indulging ourselves and exert some self-control or self-discipline.

We've all fallen short, but there's a simple remedy—genuinely repent. If Jesus is your Lord and Savior, you are no longer the sinner you used to be. The Bible calls you a New Creation— something never before seen on the earth prior to Jesus's death and resurrection. What is that New Creation? A saint.

You've moved from sinner to saint. Are you perfect? No. Does that mean you never sin again? No. But it does signify you have a choice you never had before: the decision NOT to sin. You're now a saint, who may occasionally sin.

Once sin is broken, it will no longer have a foothold.

In order to maintain our spiritual health, we must keep clean. That means regular inspections because mites hide and are often hard to find.

That mite is waiting at the door, ready to jump on your back. Don't let him in. This is a beach ball you DON'T want to play with.

Is there a cycle of sin in your life that needs to be broken?

If you do what is right, will you not be accepted? But if you do not do what is right, sin is crouching at your door; it desires to have you, but you must rule over it (Genesis 4:7).

Chapter 14 - Thou Shalt Not Steal

You shall not steal (Deuteronomy 5:19).

We had been out of town for a couple of days when I went out to the bee yard to check the hives. Agitated bees congregated in one corner of the apiary so I went in for a closer look. One of the hives was unusually silent. As I came near the hive, I saw hundreds of dead bees on the ground in front of the hive. Warning! Warning!

I lifted the lid and, sure enough, there wasn't a bee to be seen. Instead of the gentle hum that welcomes you when you open a hive, it was quiet. As I lifted each box, I became more discouraged. No bees, brood, pollen, or honey. The comb was completely empty like the halls of a high school on summer break. Finally, when I got down to the bottom of the hive, my heart sank. There they lay—thousands of bees—all dead.

Now, I know they're only bees—little flying insects with stingers. But they are my bees. And even though I can't call each one by name, I get attached to those little girls.

It was a sad day.

80

I looked at the tattered comb and immediately knew what had happened. They'd been robbed—by other bees. Believe it or not, there are "robber bees" out there. They scout out the area with their sniffers and when they get a whiff of honey, they zoom in for a free meal. Like playground bullies, they pick on weaker colonies, and once they find the honey-load, they go back and broadcast the news to the rest of their gang.

The bees at home will fight to the death to protect their honey, but without help from the beekeeper, they'll eventually lose. Once the robbers overwhelm the colony, they chew open every cell, leaving nothing behind but a graveyard of thousands of honest, hardworking bees. It's heartbreaking.

I'm sure these robber bees were once nice bees. They probably worked together and helped out around the house. But somewhere along the way something changed. They stopped cooking their own meals and started "eating out." Once they got the taste of a free meal, they went from honest hardworking bees to destructive criminals.

There's a reason God says, in His first set of guidelines, "Thou shalt not steal." He didn't lay down these rules because He was trying to spoil our fun. On the contrary, it's because He knows small sins grow into bigger ones that eventually destroy us and everyone else in the vicinity.

God wants us to be successful—the right way. Real success comes from a life well-lived within good guidelines. Because our Father loves His children, He sets boundaries for us that give us a solid structure on which we can hang the fabric of our lives. We experience the greatest fulfillment when we live from the safety of His boundaries.

On the other hand, we're rebels. We want to do what we want, when we want, and the way we want regardless of the consequences. We push back every time we hear the word "No." We learned it from Adam, and we've stubbornly stomped our foot ever since. That defiance set mankind on a road straight to Hell, so God stepped in to interrupt the downward spiral of our history.

When He established the Israelites as a nation, God gave them rules to live by. He knew their rebellion, if left unattended, would destroy them. It would leave a murky residue of man's contract with the devil to pass down from generation to generation. Our rebellion is an ongoing consequence of man's treason in the garden of Eden.

Like robber bees going after honey, the devil wants to steal everything God has given us. The enemy robs us of our joy, our health, our wealth, our peace, our relationships, and on and on it goes, moment by moment, until he has cleaned out everything, leaving nothing behind but an empty shell.

How do we know when the enemy has a foothold in our lives? Take a minute and ask yourself a few questions: Is there confusion in your life? Fear? Anxiety? Depression? Those things are from your enemy, not God.

While the devil comes to steal, kill and destroy, Jesus offers the opposite: life. And the life He offers is even greater than all we can ask or imagine.

According to Scripture, God wants us to prosper. God's blessings come, not because we deserve them, but because He expects us to share our blessings with others.

Bible teacher Derek Prince put it this way: If you need $100 a day to cover your expenses and have a little left over, God wants to give you $125 a day—so you can use your bounty to bless others.

Generosity is the opposite of greed, and greed is one of the most powerful demonic forces on the earth. If we can learn to be generous, God will bless us. In YWAM, we call that moving in the opposite spirit. When you're faced with greed, give. You can't out-give God. The more you give, the more He gives to you because He knows He can trust you with abundance.

However, Jesus' alternative does come with boundaries. Let's stop believing the lie that the ends justify the means. If we would simply listen to our King, our lives, like the hive, would be productive and fulfilling. And, regardless of what the world says, when it comes down to it, who could ask for more? Let's stop saying "No" to the Father who really does know best.

And, instead of looking for a free meal, why not try cooking at home?

How has the devil been stealing from you? What can you do to stop it?

The thief comes only to steal and kill and destroy; I have come that they may have life, and have it to the full (John 10:10).

Chapter 15 - Bearding

Then God blessed the seventh day and made it holy, because on it he rested from all the work of creating that he had done (Genesis 2:2-3).

It was a warm evening early in July when I walked through the bee yard to find a large cluster of bees almost covering the entire front of one of the hives. The bees were clinging together right above the entrance, toe to toe and antenna to antenna, so tightly packed it looked like the hive had a beard. Beekeepers call this BEEhavior "bearding." Clever.

No one really knows why bees act like that. It usually happens when the weather is warm or if they're preparing to swarm. I looked around and none of the other colonies were bearding, so I made a note to check on this one daily. Sure enough, every afternoon around 4:00 the bees would begin gathering on the front of the hive. It looked like they were relaxing.

Bees don't have eyelids, so they don't sleep the way we do, but they do rest. By bearding they're out of the way of the bees working inside, and they can relax outside where the temperature is cooler. Like my grandparents used to do, they're sitting on the porch enjoying the breeze and watching the world go by. Ahh, the good ole days!

Since I'm reminiscing a bit, do you remember when everything shut down on Sundays? You may not be old enough, but I am. We couldn't even buy milk on Sunday, much less go to a movie. In my family if we wanted entertainment, we read the Sunday morning comics or went for a drive. Those were the lazy days of summer when families adjourned to the front porch after dinner, sharing stories and visiting with neighbors who stopped by. We kids climbed the giant maple tree in the front yard or rode our Schwinn one-speed bicycles through the empty streets waiting for the lightning bugs to start twinkling.

Sounds like life in Mayberry,[29] doesn't it? Life seemed simpler and slower. But honestly, do we really want to go back to the days of no air conditioning, computers, or cellphones? Most of us would say, "No." Electronics give us instant information, instant communication, and instant entertainment. We literally have the world at our fingertips.

Those conveniences are wonderful but they also come with a price. We save time, but generate more work. We have more stuff, but need more stuff to take care of the stuff we have. Our calendars are full, but we don't enjoy the moment. We've perfected the art of multi-tasking, but have lost the ability to focus. We're in a hurry, but we don't know why.

The beat of the drummer we march to gets faster and faster until we're running to catch up. But, catch up to what? We balance a hamburger in one hand and our cellphone in the other as we exit the drive-through because we don't have time to sit down to a meal—even at a fast food restaurant!

It seems those bearding bees know when to take a break. Do we?

Because He made it all, God understands the frailty of His people and the world. He modeled the idea of rest on the seventh day of creation, and when the Israelites moved in to the Promised Land, God even commanded them to let the land rest every seven years.[30] They didn't, so He removed them and sent them into exile. Sounds like He's pretty serious about this Sabbath thing.

When you're an agrarian society, and God tells you to take a year off from farming, there's bound to be some pushback. That would mean trusting Him to provide everything for two years— the sabbatical year and the following one because it would take another year for the new crops to come in.

Taking a rest really challenges our faith. It says, "Okay, God, You've got this. I'm trusting You."

Doctors agree that rest, along with a proper diet and exercise, plays an essential role in our well-being. It's a time of physical healing and mental renewal.

Both God and the enemy understand the power of rest, which is why God commands it and the enemy attacks it. When I'm tired, I have less grace for others. My temper is shorter, and my productivity takes longer.

Yet we still don't rest, even though God commanded it. Oh, sure, we may not be "working," but we're still not resting. Let's face it, the weekend seems to be the only time we have to work around the house. We mow the lawn, wash clothes, trim the bushes, haul the kids to the game, vacuum, shop for groceries, go to church, paint the fence, answer our emails, pay the bills, plan the meals, update our Facebook page, and wash the car. Whew! I'm tired just writing all that down! (That reminds me, I have a few things to do ... Uhh, never mind.)

Don't get me wrong. I know those things have to be done. But, when do we rest? Jesus said, "The Sabbath was made for man, not man for the Sabbath." In other words, "Take a break!" We all need to recharge our batteries. And the best way I know is to start building in a time of rest during the week, whether it's a little time each day or a whole afternoon of simply chillin'.

So, let's step back into the sepia tones of yesterday and breathe some fresh air. Why don't you pour yourself a nice tall glass of sweet tea, or whatever you like, and join me on the porch for a while? We'll listen to the crickets, watch the birds, and share our funniest stories while we greet the neighbors passing by.

There's an empty rocking chair for you, and I'm sure it won't be long before God stops by for a visit too.

What are some ways you can build a Sabbath into your week?

Be still, and know that I am God (Psalm. 46:10).

Chapter 16 - Burn, Baby, Burn

And when you stand praying, if you hold anything against anyone, forgive them, so that your Father in heaven may forgive you your sins (Mark 11:25).

I love a campfire. The smell of wood-burning smoke circling upward and drifting off to parts unknown is somehow comforting. Yet, there's no comfort today. No matter how I position myself, the smoke attacks my eyes and permeates my clothes and hair as I toss old waxed frames into the fire.

It's never fun to burn bee equipment—especially frames of drawn honeycomb. The bees worked hard to generate that wax and shape it into perfect hexagons—and now it's going up in flames. Still, sometimes burning frames is necessary.

Even when the hives are located in pesticide-free zones like ours, microscopic contaminants float through the air and eventually end up in the wax. Like old sponges soak up germs, affected comb can contribute to poor health in the colony.

Bees keep a clean house. They're also efficient and reuse honeycomb. When a baby bee first emerges from her cell, she cleans it, like making her own bed, so it will be ready for another egg, honey or pollen—whatever the colony needs. As the comb is used again and again, the once pearly white wax becomes darker. The darker the wax, the more polluted it is with tiny amounts of chemicals unintentionally brought in by the bees.

The solution? Put fresh frames in the hive and take out the old comb and burn it. So, here I am standing around a hot fire, thinking about God's lesson for today.

As beekeepers remove old comb to keep the hive in tip-top shape, Christ-followers stay healthy spiritually by letting go of past offenses. Every day we have the opportunity to become offended: the boss who gave you the stay-after-work-to-get-it-done assignment; the teacher who embarrassed you in front of your classmates; your parents (don't roll your eyes) or your spouse or brother who's, well, breathing. (That was a joke.)

What I'm talking about is unforgiveness. Like being locked in on a Ferris wheel with no way to get off, we're constantly moving, but going nowhere. When we hold onto offenses, unforgiveness takes root and bitterness moves in. Our worldview can become colored by suspicion where no one is trustworthy and everyone has an ulterior motive.

When we refuse to forgive, we're held captive in a self-made prison. We cover up the bars with nice linen curtains, replace the metal cot with a comfortable sofa, add a rug and pictures on the wall, and tell ourselves we're okay. However, the bars are still there and the dirt is still under the rug. Unforgiveness is quiet and grows underground until that little pile of dust has become a mountain the size of an elephant in the middle of the room.

Like a cancer growing unforgiveness extends its spidery tentacles into every corner of our lives. But Jesus has a cure for this cancer. Actually, He became the cure when He laid aside His God-ness and became human to bridge the gap between God and mankind.

Jesus taught about forgiveness and modeled it on the cross saying, "Father, forgive them." But He wasn't only talking about ruthless Romans and pious priests. He was also looking forward through history and forgiving us. Forgiveness is a cornerstone of the Kingdom.

While society promotes revenge and paybacks, God, who is just, advocates forgiveness. It's so important to Him that in Matthew 5:24 Jesus says, "If you are offering your gift at the altar and there remember that your brother or sister has something against you, leave your gift there in front of the altar. First, go and be reconciled to them; then come and offer your gift."

Later on in Matthew 6:12 when His disciples ask Him to teach them to pray, Jesus includes forgiveness in the prayer saying, "Forgive us our debts, as we also have forgiven our debtors."

We like the "forgive us" part. But we tend to skim over "as we forgive others." We know we need forgiveness, but we're not so willing to extend it to others.

In the sermon in Matthew 7:1, Jesus tells us not to judge others because we'll be judged by God with the same measure we use against others. Then He gives His famous illustration of focusing on the speck in your neighbor's eye while ignoring the log in your own eye.

What I hear Jesus saying in these passages is that if I'm not willing to forgive, I shouldn't even bother praying because God's not listening.

I see the logic. Why should I pray to God when I've already set myself on His throne by judging others? I'm not qualified to bring judgment.

As we take a step back from Jesus's words, we get a better picture: Jesus talks about forgiveness, He teaches us to pray, then He speaks about forgiveness again. I see a theme developing here.

Forgiveness is the bread that bookends the meat of our prayers to God.

When Suki and I teach on "Forgiveness," we ask the class if they need to forgive anyone. They make a list on paper while we light a fire. When everyone is ready, they bring their lists to burn. Some crumple the pages and toss them into the fire while others quietly offer them to the flame then watch the paper being consumed. It's a holy moment.

Forgiveness is a choice. It doesn't depend upon how you feel or who deserves what. It doesn't justify what happened nor does it excuse wrongdoing. It does, however, release us from bondage so healing can begin.

May I suggest it's time to let go? Let go of the old contaminated memories of your past. Those archives are dark, like the comb, and they're unhealthy.

So why don't you join me around the fire pit? You can strike the match!

Is there someone you need to forgive today?

Do not judge, and you will not be judged. Do not condemn, and you will not be condemned. Forgive, and you will be forgiven (Luke 6:37).

Chapter 17 - Sometimes There Is No Answer

And we know that in all things God works for the good of those who love him, who have been called according to his purpose (Romans 8:28).

Winter in Tennessee is predictably unpredictable. It's not unusual to have temperatures climb into the 60's for a few days in January or February. And this year, as if right on cue, around the first of February we had a week-long break from the cold. So I threw on my jacket and ventured out to the bee yard to check on the girls. Sure enough, some bees were out flying again.

One by one, I inspected the entrance of each hive looking for action. The more activity I see, the stronger the hive. The stronger the hive, the better their chance of surviving the winter. I was pleased to see these mid-winter signs of life. I began my examination of the first row. *So far, so good.* The second row of hives also looked promising as I saw more bees venturing out from their cozy clusters.

Bees were flying in the last row, too, until I came to the last hive.

98

Nothing. No buzzing bees were peeking out the front door. My heart sank—again. I know, they're only bees and I shouldn't grow attached, but—as I've said before— they're MY bees! I lifted the lid. Silence. I looked down between the frames. Nothing. I took off the first box. Still no sign of life.

Sometimes a beekeeper has to put on a deerstalker cap like Sherlock Holmes and search for clues. I didn't put on the hat, but I did re-examine the frames. Not a bee to be found. *They hadn't frozen.* Check. Honey and pollen still in the comb. Check. *They hadn't been robbed.* No dead bees in a tiny cluster head first in the comb. *They hadn't starved.* Check. Elementary, my dear Watson, the bees have simply vanished (dramatic music plays)—into thin air!

Time to do some research. I headed back to the warmth of the house and rifled through my records looking for any past unusual behavior in that hive. I combed through their history for an explanation. Everything seemed normal. I looked for clues in the array of bee books on my overstuffed bookshelves. Nothing. Finally, I picked up the phone and sought advice from a beekeeping mentor.

He listened to my sad story. I could almost see him nodding as I described the scene. Then, I waited—knowing his sage advice would solve my mystery. "Well," he sighed, "sometimes there is no answer. Bees just do what bees are going to do."

Well, that didn't help! I was hoping for some expansive homespun explanation that would bring some comfort or at least understanding. Instead I got, "Well, bees just do what bees are going to do." *Seriously?*

Have you ever felt that way with God? I have. *God, I need an answer! Why are You so silent?* Over the years I've stopped asking "Why?" because I've learned God is going to do what He's going to do. No matter how hard I look for an answer, He doesn't have to give me one. He's God, and I'm not.

God is described as sovereign over 290 times in the Bible. We call Him King and Lord, but in the United States we really don't understand the idea of Sovereignty. In a democracy, the government operates by the will and vote of the people. Government representatives are supposed to answer to the people who elected them. If we don't like what they're doing, we can vote them out of office. In a democracy every vote counts and every opinion matters. Majority rules. So we form committees and debate issues and try to come to a compromise that will keep everyone happy.

A kingdom is on the opposite end of the government scale. In a kingdom the vote of the people means nothing and only one opinion matters—the king's. When a king makes a ruling, it's not up for discussion. His ruling is law and it demands obedience. Do you see where I'm going here?

God is God. We didn't elect Him. And we can't vote Him out of office.

If we want to be effective citizens of His Kingdom, we can't continue to think democratically. God's sovereignty was established in the first sentence of the Bible when He created the heavens and the earth, and it will continue throughout all eternity.

But God's rulership is not hard. We can be confident because we have a good King. Scripture says He rules with justice and mercy. He's loving and kind.

I think we sometimes confuse God's sovereignty with Greek mythology. Remember Zeus? He was known for "playing games" with people. He toyed with humans like we dangle a toy in front of a kitten, keeping the prize just out of reach. If Zeus was in a bad mood, the people on the earth suffered.

Our sovereign God doesn't play games with us, and He doesn't punish us because He's in a bad mood. Actually, God never wakes up on the wrong side of the bed. Love can't.

God's position is this: He is sovereign, and His authority is absolute. God's essence is this: He is love, and He rules us from Who He is.

Isaiah and Jeremiah say God is the potter, and we are the clay. So He gets to decide how He will mold us and what type of vessels we will be.[31]

His decisions are carefully governed by what is best for each of us. He gives us desires, then helps us achieve them. The Potter makes us into the perfect vessels so we can be fulfilled and accomplish our purpose.

We clap our hands and sing "You are the Potter …", but all too often, we want to tell God what He should do with our lives. We want to have a vote—and we want answers.

I never found my "lost" bees. I suspect their disappearance was what we call Colony Collapse Disorder— a mysterious epidemic in the world of beekeeping where the bees disappear, leaving the beekeeper scratching his head. Either that or they decided to move to another home. My beekeeping mentor was right. I won't always know the answer, because sometimes bees just do what bees are going to do.

And, sometimes God does too.

Have you ever cried out, "God, where are you?" Has He ever told you, "His grace is sufficient?"

In you, LORD my God, I put my trust (Psalm 25:1).

Chapter 18 - Standing Up to the Giants

"Give me a 15-foot crocodile any day over a bee." — Bindi Irwin

Guard bees. Every hive has them. They're the ones who buzz around your head harassing unprotected visitors until they run for cover. When a guard bee stings you, she releases an alarm pheromone that tells everyone in the hive there's a danger. As the distress signal spreads, more bees drop their chores and head into battle—it's a call to arms. And while you may be bigger, if you wage war with one of these lookouts, you'll probably end up breaking the record for the 100-yard dash.

When guard bees aren't flying in your face, they're doing sentry duty at the hive's entrance. These patrolling officers inspect every approaching bee. Those who don't smell like the family are quickly surrounded by the troops and forcibly removed.

These lion-hearted soldiers know the safety of the hive rests on their tiny shoulders and they are prepared to do battle with any threat, even from a giant like me. You won't catch them napping! So, when one starts bullying me, I give her room, because I've been driven from the apiary more than once by these diligent defenders.

King Solomon says we need to be diligent, too. He says, "Above all else guard your heart," but he's not talking about putting up walls to keep people out. He's talking about inspecting everything that comes in to make sure it smells right.

Sour-smelling lies are the giants invading our land, and we need to stand up to them. They attack our identity, our sense of value and eventually, replace the truth. Unfortunately, some thoughts have been with us so long, they've become part of our core values. But those old lies need to be replaced with God's truth. Then those giants will begin to fall.

We start by examining our own self-talk. Some thoughts are corrosive and undermine our relationships with family, friends, and God. Here are some examples: "I can't trust anyone," "I'm so stupid," "I'll never amount to anything." Even magazines, Facebook, and television pile onto our low self-esteem with stories like "Ten Ways to Improve Your ... Whatever."

Remember the story of David and Goliath? Goliath was a 9-foot-tall Philistine soldier, who was taunting the Israelite army. David was a teenager delivering a boxed lunch to his brothers (my version). When he overheard Goliath's insults, he thought, *Who does this guy think he is? He's challenging the armies of the living God* (again, my version).

So David accepted the challenge. He wasn't a soldier. He was a shepherd with no armor, no training, and no sword. His only weapon was a slingshot and a few small stones. Yet he did something amazing. Instead of running away, he ran toward this armored-up giant and threw his first stone. It hit Goliath in the middle of his forehead, and he was felled like a mammoth redwood in the forest. Oh, I forgot to mention—David also had God on his side.

I love this story because David wasn't a superhero. He didn't have special powers like Superman or cool custom-made armor like Batman. He didn't even have "spidey-senses." He was simply a regular guy—with God on his side.

We all face giants, A to Z. May I introduce you to a few? They are addictions, bullying, criticism, divorce, economic crises, financial failure, guilt, hatred, illnesses, jealousy, killing, lying—and I could continue all the way to "zombies." There's an alphabet soup of pain in the world, and Satan is stirring the pot. Can you smell it?

Giants are enormous and intimidating, so they're easy to see. Yet because they are so big, we forget they started out as little lies that weren't taken captive in our minds. Evil is not an inanimate force that hits some of us and misses others. It's a targeted attack from our enemy, Satan, and it usually begins with a lie.

In John 8:44, Jesus is talking to the Pharisees saying, "You belong to your father, the devil, and you want to carry out your father's desires. He was a murderer from the beginning, not holding to the truth, there is no truth in him. When he lies, he speaks his native language, for he is a liar and the father of lies."

As we look through the Bible, we see the enemy lies about three things: God, himself and us.

Satan wants to destroy our relationship with God, so his first tactic is to lie about who God is. He began that strategy in the garden with Eve, causing her to doubt God's goodness.

He also wants to confuse us regarding who he is. In 2 Corinthians 11:14, Paul tells us that Satan masquerades as an angel of light. He wants us to believe one of two tenets: he's as powerful as God or he doesn't exist.

Finally, Satan lies to us about us. He wants us to believe we don't matter, or we aren't important. Or he wants us to think we're all that matters. Either way, he has effectively caused us to put ourselves first.

Recognizing the enemy's lies is the initial step toward reorienting our lives so we can become confident in who God is and who we are. Once we get that order right, we can readily recognize the enemy's voice.

Like the guard bees do with each approaching bee, let's practice sniffing out each incoming thought to see if we should let it stay.

Once we recognize who the giant is, God tightens the laces on our boxing gloves and urges us into the middle of the ring. Yes, we're in the ring, but we can look back and see He's still in our corner, smiling! We don't even have to throw a punch. All we have to do is stand our ground.

We don't need a bat-mobile or a superhero's cape—just some pebbles and ... good sniffers.

What are some lies that grew to become giants in your life?

I have given you authority to trample on snakes and scorpions and to overcome all the power of the enemy; nothing will harm you (Luke 10:19).

Chapter 19 - Stuck Like Glue

Now faith is confidence in what we hope for and assurance about what we do not see (Hebrews 11:1).

I washed my bee suit the other day. After working with the bees all summer it was looking dingy. My once pristine white jacket looked like I had been rolling in the mud. The front and sleeves were stained a dark reddish brown and no matter how hard I scrubbed, the sticky stuff wouldn't come off. So much for winning a beekeeper's fashion contest!

So what is this sticky stuff? Actually, it's another product from the hive.

Besides the delicious honey and multifunctional wax, bees also make glue. That's right, glue. Beekeepers often call it "bee glue," however the proper name is propolis. Bees collect resin from buds and sap that are part of a tree's immune system. Once it's in the bees' stomachs, different enzymes are added to make a gummy cocktail they can use to glue everything together. Propolis also fights bacteria, viruses, and fungi that would otherwise pose a threat to the colony.

Because of its healing properties, propolis is now being sold to humans. It's reported to cure everything from pimples to cancer. Check your local health food store for details.

The bees also use propolis to fill and seal crevices and gaps, smooth over rough wood and even encase objects too large to carry out of the hive. For example, if a mouse is unlucky enough to try to make the inside of a hive its home, the bees will kill it and completely encase it in propolis so the decaying mouse can't spread disease in the hive.

For beekeepers, dealing with propolis is frustrating. This "glue" is so strong you can't pull it apart with your hands. You need the leverage of a hive tool to pry things apart. You could say bees make the glue that holds everything together.

For Christ-followers, faith is that glue. Faith holds on when everyone else says, "Let it go." Faith swims against the current like the woman who had been bleeding for 12 years. She fought through the crowd, paddling against the cultural protocol of the day. She was unclean and couldn't touch anyone. She didn't care. "If I only touch (Jesus') cloak, I will be healed."[32] Faith drove her, held her together, gave her the boldness to act, and healed her!

Faith, not need, is what moves the hand of God. Don't believe me? Look at what moved Jesus. In Luke 18 we see Jesus passing through the streets of Jericho. He walked right past a blind beggar sitting on the roadside who had to cry out and call after Jesus to get His attention—not an easy task for a blind man. His faith stirred him to swim upstream, and, according to Jesus, his faith healed him.

None of us start out with great faith. It grows as we use it, like a muscle. Jesus says even a little faith can move mountains. So I suggest we try it. When someone's in pain, instead of offering an aspirin, let's pray first. They might not need that aspirin after all.

As we begin to exercise our faith, it will get stronger. We'll have more confidence. As our confidence grows, we'll have greater faith to pray for blind eyes to see, deaf ears to hear, and maybe, even the dead raised to life. After all, isn't that what Jesus told us to do? He said, "Heal the sick, cleanse the lepers, cast out demons, and raise the dead."

That's a pretty tall order, but Jesus made a declaration of faith we can grow into. His disciples, who according to Jesus, had little faith, asked Him to increase their faith. Jesus' response was they only needed a little—the size of a mustard seed— to do the work of the Kingdom.

When I was a new Christ-follower and on a roller coaster ride with Jesus, my pastor gave me a pin that had a mustard seed in it. I wore it daily as a reminder that I didn't need a lot of faith—but I did need some. I couldn't be faithless, nor could I be independent.

I needed a faith that would hold me together when I had to swim upstream.

One of my first swims took me on a long journey upriver when God called me to the mission field. By the world's standards, I was doing fine. I had a home and my own business. I was active in the community and in my church. My social calendar was booked, my family was well, and my future looked good. I was swimming with the current and moving downstream at a steady pace along with everyone else.

Then God stepped in and called me to missions. And, frankly, I wanted to hang up my floaties and step out of the water. Instead, I started doing the backstroke. I splashed and thrashed around in the water for a while but the tide was shifting, and I was losing my buoyancy.

God was asking me to change course and start swimming upstream. That meant swimming against the current, and I didn't want to go.

It took a year, but I finally mustered up the faith to close my business. A friend moved into my house, and I said a tearful goodbye to my friends and family.

Swimming upstream has its challenges, but it also has its advantages: blind men get their sight, lame men walk, bleeding women get healed, and sometimes someone answers God's call.

A little faith goes a long way.

I want faith that sticks like glue, and, like propolis, won't wash off. How about you?

Would you say that you have strong faith? What can you do to increase it?

For we live by faith, not by sight (2 Corinthians 5:7).

Chapter 20 - Baby, It's Cold Outside

Those who hope in the Lord will renew their strength. They will soar on wings like eagles, they will run and not grow weary, they will walk and not be faint (Isaiah 40:31).

Brrrr. There's such a heavy frost on the ground this morning it looks like it has snowed. And here I sit with my first cup of coffee—by the fire. That's right. I'm not outside watching the bees; I'm inside where it's warm. In case you didn't catch it—it's cold outside! Even country girls know to stay inside when the weather's bad. So, I'm enjoying the flames as they dance above the logs. Besides, there's nothing for me to do in the bee yard.

Folks often ask me "What do the bees do in the winter? Do they hibernate like bears or are they simply sleeping?" The answer is, "No, they're not sleeping."

It's easy to think that. On the outside, a hive in the winter looks like an empty box standing alone in a forgotten field. There aren't any bees flying around, and there's no sound inside. If you put your hands on the walls of the hive, it would be as cold as everything else outside.

Yet, as forlorn as a winter hive looks, there's life inside the box. The bees are still working, we just can't see it. When temperatures drop and the days get shorter, the queen lays fewer and fewer eggs and may even stop laying for a while.

Instead of raising more brood, the bees shift into a survival mode. They form a tight cluster around the queen and any unhatched brood, and they begin to vibrate their little bodies. This movement raises the temperature in the cluster to around 93 degrees which keeps the brood alive and everyone else warm. Even if it's five degrees below zero outside, the bees stay toasty in their self-made sauna.

The bees on the outside of the cluster act as insulators. When they get cold, they move deeper into the bee ball while those in the center take their turn on the outer edge.

Except for the queen, there's a constant rotation of bees in the cluster.

The bees aren't trying to keep the entire hive warm, which is why the box is still cold to the touch. So, even though I may not see any activity outside the hive, I know the bees are still busy.

And, likewise, when my relationship with God gets quiet, I know He's not idle either. Sometimes ministry slows down and opportunities to serve dry up. Other times it's hard to read the

Bible daily, and often my prayer life seems to turn into "sounds of silence."[33]

That's when it gets hard. It feels like my heart has been chilled. I need a soft Jesus blanket to wrap around me and someone to pat me on the shoulder and say "It's okay. You'll get through this."

It's easy to become discouraged on those cold winter nights. That's when I learn to trust God the most, believing He's preparing me for something I can't see further down the road.

The Bible calls it "walking by faith and not by sight." And that's not easy when, in spite of my prayers, I can't see any change in my circumstances. I struggle to keep putting one foot in front of the other. Frankly, it feels like I'm walking in knee-deep snow without snowshoes.

I remind myself we have seasons in our lives like the seasons in nature. These rhythms are a critical part of our growth. Even though I see leafless trees outside, I know things are happening below the frosty surface. Roots are growing.

God designed every season, even quiet ones like winter, and when He tells me, "Be still," I struggle, though I know it's too cold outside to do much else. So I sit, obediently, and try not to squirm, because I know the underground growth draws us closer to the Wonderful One who created us.

While activity is good for us, we've lost the skill of sitting still with God.

Bible teacher Donna Jordon gives a graphic illustration of busyness. The Chinese language is written with pictures for words, rather than letters. The picture for the word busyness is a combination of two pictures: one of the heart and the other of death. The meaning is clear: Heart-dead.

We can become so consumed with work or activities that we allow our hearts to become calloused to family, friends, even God. We're so "plugged in" we have our phones programmed to alert us to every Facebook post, News Feed, email or Tweet that flutters across our screen—urgent business that requires us to be available 24/7!

We're easily distracted, and we've let those habits carry over to our quiet times with God. If we're not careful, we'll drift too far away from the warmth of fellowship with Him.

We've become a society that's afraid to be still. Addicted to the "white noise" of electronics, we quickly become bored if we have to sit in a meeting for more than 90 minutes. We're uncomfortable with silence, so we have to fill it with something.

God won't compete with the distractions from the world. He's God and He has the right to demand my full attention. So I deliberately get away from the noise, and I wait on Him. I have my journal and a pen ready to write down the thoughts and impressions He gives me. I lay down my agenda and open my heart to what He wants to say.

It's not a burning bush; it's a fire in the wood stove. I'm not on a mountaintop; I'm sitting with my Bible in hand and my feet before the fire.

Here I am Lord. I'm listening.

How does God get your attention? Do you make time to simply listen to Him?

Be still before the LORD and wait patiently for him (Psalm 37:7).

Chapter 21 - Where Are We?

For we are God's handiwork, created in Christ Jesus to do good works, which God prepared in advance for us to do (Ephesians 2:10).

It's about 3:00 in the afternoon, and I watch as one by one they tentatively emerge from the hive—hundreds of them. These are the young bees getting ready to take their first orientation flights. Before the flying begins, each one seems to go through the ritual of walking along the surface of the hive, like they're memorizing every nuance of the wood.

Soon these little bees take to the air. When they do, they will only fly out a few inches and immediately turn back to face the hive, maneuvering in tight figure-eight patterns in front of the entrance. They're not looking outward—at least not yet. They're studying the hive, using all their senses, especially the sense of smell, as they learn the look and feel of home. Even when hives are standing close to one another, the bees don't get confused.

Gradually, their figure eight patterns start growing larger and larger as the bees begin flying

122

above the hive and all the way around it. They're exploring the neighborhood and the surrounding terrain. They're mentally cataloging elevations in the land and other landmarks like trees and nearby buildings. Soon I'll lose sight of them as they take their first solo flight.

Like the bees, as children of God we need the right orientation. Our assignment is to know God before we can make Him known.[34] So how do we do that? There's a LOT to learn about God. And, how do we know when we're ready to venture out?

Stepping out can be frightening, so like the bees we orient ourselves by studying our home. And for the Christ-follower, "home" is Jesus. He is the doorway to our faith and the foundation on which it's built. He's the exact representation of the Father. Jesus says, "If you've seen me, you've seen the Father." So, if our view of God doesn't line up with the Person of Jesus, we've picked up some wrong theology somewhere.

Like future foragers using all their senses to examine their home, we begin by learning to taste and see that the Lord is good. As bees memorize key characteristics of the hive, we should memorize some key Scriptures to keep us oriented properly.

Knowing Scripture will deposit truth in our hearts, and that truth, with the guidance and counsel of the Holy Spirit, will keep us from getting lost. He is like a built-in GPS telling us when to turn and when to go straight.

As we become oriented, God begins to send us farther out. We may feel totally inadequate, but I think He enjoys using unlikely people to advance His Kingdom. He never sends us out prematurely, and He always goes before us to prepare the way.[35]

At age 13, I boarded a plane for the first time. I was going to visit my aunt and uncle in Washington, D.C. for the summer—and I was alone. Nervousness and excitement competed for dominance in my heart as Mom walked me to the gate (in those days you could) and kissed me goodbye. I stepped out of my comfort zone and onto the plane.

That was my first big adventure. I was on my own, but still connected to home by family. I was independent, yet I talked to Mom every night. I was circling farther away from my nest, but I knew where home was.

You have to be willing to go where you've never been in order to get what you've never had. For a couple of months, I tasted a whole new world, rich with history and beauty in our nation's capital.

At the end of the summer, I returned home bubbling over with tales of my adventures and photo albums filled with pictures taken with my Kodak Brownie camera. But I came back with more than photos. I brought home a new confidence and courage to step out beyond my own borders.

That first journey set me up to board another plane 30 years later. Again, I would be alone, headed for an adventure even farther away from my comfort zone. This time I was headed to Hawaii and the mission field.

My confidence level was higher this time, but I have to admit, halfway over the Pacific Ocean, I was having second thoughts. That is until I got reoriented by calling home. I opened my Bible and God answered the phone. There it was ... Isaiah 49:6: "I will also make you a light for the Gentiles, that you may bring my salvation to the ends of the earth."

That was the beginning of a trip that forever changed me. And I'm still bubbling over with tales of the amazing things I have seen and the wonderful people I've come to know.

Is it time for you to take a look around and step out of your comfort zone? You'll feel the warmth of the sun on your face, a gentle breeze in your hair, and you'll realize it's not so bad out there after all. That first step is always a bit scary because, like the bee, once you start flapping your wings, your feet will leave the ground. It's exhilarating and frightening all at the same time.

If your heart drops down to your stomach at the thought of boarding the plane, keep your eyes on home because once you take off, you'll never be the same again.

Why don't you join me? I promise, you'll enjoy the flight.

Is your GPS working? What's your next step? What does that look like?

For we live by faith, not by sight (2 Corinthians 5:7).

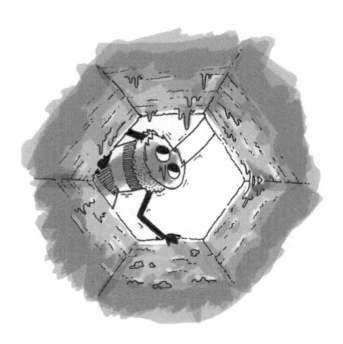

Chapter 22 - Where Did all the Honey Go?

"The busy bee has no time for sorrow." — William Blake

It was harvest time. We were excited. This is what we'd been working for all year—honey. Earlier in the spring Suki and I had added extra supers so the bees could fill them with excess honey. Then we left them alone. We monitored the hives by watching the entrances and, sure enough, bees zipped in and out like they'd been shot out of a cannon. The bees looked good! Go, girls, go!

Then July came and the honey flow was over. It was hot and the rain had moved to Florida. Flowers stopped blooming, the clover dried up, and the grass turned brown. The bees had gleaned all they could from Mother Nature until the fall.

It was our turn. The honey on our shelves from last year was gone and our customers were clamoring for this year's harvest. Most beekeepers are hobbyists, like us, but because there's usually a surplus of honey, we also sell it.

We uncovered the honey extractor and cleaned all the equipment. We set up tables and

128

buckets, washed the bottles and checked the labels. We were ready and excited. Did I say that already? We eagerly zipped up our suits and grabbed our equipment as we headed to the hives.

We lifted the lid and peered inside the first box like excited children on Christmas morning ...

What? Wait a minute. Where's the honey? We stared dumbly at the empty frames in the top box. The bees were fine. They had enough honey to get them through the coming winter (almost 50 pounds), but there wasn't any extra for us. *Well, this hive was a small colony.*

Disappointment tried to creep in, but we kept it at bay as we gently closed the lid on hive number one. Every colony is different and some don't produce as much honey as others. *Not to worry.* We rationalized. *We've got other hives.* We turned to hive number two, then number three, then four—a pattern was developing.

One by one we approached each hive with shrinking enthusiasm. Only a few of them had any extra honey at all. As we moved through the apiary, it was clear we weren't going to get the harvest we had hoped for this year.

My thoughts raced: *We won't have enough honey for our customers—or ourselves.* Next: *What have I done wrong that the bees aren't producing?* And finally: *Maybe I should give up beekeeping altogether.* Discouragement pushed harder.

Have your thoughts ever spiraled down to "the pit?" That day mine did. We've all had bad days, in varying degrees—from minor disappointments to major tragedies. And every incident can bring discouragement, grief, pain, or rejection into our lives. That's when it's hard to get out of bed, hard to be around people, and hard to keep going.

Sometimes when life knocks you down, you don't want to get up. I understand. I was ready to give up on my bees. However, no matter what our circumstances, we can't let discouragement rob us of our faith. Disappointment is like a speed bump in the road. We can't stop the car, get out and walk away when we come to it—we have to go over that hump. Sure, it will slow us down a bit, but how we deal with those bumps determines how far down the road we'll get.

David was discouraged, too. In fact, he'd had a bad day—for years. Let me fill you in: King Saul was already on the throne when the teenager, David, was anointed king of Israel, and Saul was jealous. He often tried to kill David, who ended up hiding in the desert for over ten years with a band of more than 600 misfits.

They settled in enemy territory, in a town called Ziklag, because they weren't safe in their own country. From there they fought as mercenaries for the Philistines. One day while they were away fighting, a raiding party of Amalekites attacked Ziklag, burned it to the ground, took their livestock, and captured their wives and children. When the men returned home to discover the tragedy, David's friends turned their anger on him and wanted to stone him! I'd say that's a bad day!

David could have walked away when he hit that bump in the road, but he didn't. Instead, he turned to God and "encouraged himself in the Lord" (1 Samuel 30:6, KJV). When life delivers an unexpected blow, we have a choice. We can whine, get angry, give up, or ... choose to turn to God. Only He can be our protection and our refuge at the same time.[36]

David and his men chased after the unsuspecting Amalekites and destroyed them, recovering everything that had been taken—and more.

Eventually, David became the most famous king in Israel's history, yet he always knew where his strength came from—not his army, his wealth, his position, nor his status. David's strength came from the Lord, and he sang about it over and over in the Psalms.

I, too, am learning to lean on Him in my distress. When I run low on fuel, God's strength keeps me from getting stuck on that bump of discouragement. I kept my faith that day, and I didn't quit beekeeping. I didn't even kick over a hive.

Later on I learned all the beekeepers in my area had huge honey losses, too. The rainy spring weather which washed away the nectar in the flowers was the culprit. My customers were disappointed, but they understood, and will be looking forward to next summer when, hopefully, we'll have all the honey we want.

Perhaps you've faced a time more discouraging than losing a business. How did you handle it?

But David found strength in the LORD his God (1 Samuel 30:6).

Chapter 23 - Cleanliness Is Next to ...

Let us draw near to God with a sincere heart and with the full assurance that faith brings, having our hearts sprinkled to cleanse us from a guilty conscience and having our bodies washed with pure water (Hebrews 10:22).

Cleanliness is next to godliness. Ever heard that one?

I'm mulling over the thought as I pull up a chair by the hives. I like to watch the late afternoon activity at the hive's entrance. The bees ignore me as they go about their daily duties, totally focused on the task at hand. Some patrol the entrance while others fly in and out like cargo planes bringing in fresh produce for the hive. I enjoy watching my girls and if I wait long enough, every once in a while I will see one taking out the trash.

That's right. Bees are fastidious when it comes to keeping the house clean. They remove anything that doesn't belong in the hive, whether it's a scrap of paper or a blade of grass. They're better housekeepers than I am! (Please don't look at the dust under my bed.)

Talk about clean. When a bee dies inside the hive, housemaids take off their aprons and put on their undertaker clothes to remove the body. With Herculean strength one of these girls will pull her sister's mortal remains out the door, then pick up the corpse and fly up to 100 yards away before unceremoniously dropping the deceased in the nearby field. Her objective is to get the dead body as far away from home as possible.

These girls are not the least bit interested in how things look outside the hive. They don't care if the weeds need trimming by the entrance, if the paint is peeling on the sides of the boxes or whether or not the boxes are in a straight line. They intuitively understand what really matters is that things are clean on the inside.

Jesus addressed this issue with the Pharisees, the religious leaders in the temple. He called them whitewashed tombs because they presented an outward appearance of cleanliness, but were internally corrupt.

Today, we've picked up the Pharisees' robes, put them on, and come under their influence. Scripture calls that behavior Religion. We clean up and dress up and put on our "happy face" for an hour or two on Sunday, but on the inside there's still a pile of dirt we haven't gotten to. So, we sweep it into the corner and close the door.

When I was growing up we had a "Junk Room." Company was never allowed in and the door was always shut. It started out as a sewing/craft room with lots of mismatched furniture. But gradually it became a catch-all for the extra things we knew we would eventually "need," but never really used. Eventually it became so crowded we could barely open the door. We needed to take out the trash.

Let's face it, it's easy to cover up the trash in the corners of our hearts—especially if we were raised in church. We've memorized the responsive readings: "God is good ... all the time," "How are you? ... Blessed and highly favored," but deep inside we need Someone to take out the trash.

You see, God is more concerned with the condition of our hearts than anything else.

King David knew that maintaining a right standing with God meant adjusting his heart, not only his actions. But David couldn't clean his own heart. He needed God's helping hand because a heart-washing is a supernatural event. When God does the scrubbing, it's incredibly gentle. And best of all, it's complete. Like the bees, He removes every bit of debris clogging our heart. A clean heart is God's desire for all of us.

When we look in Revelation at the end of the Bible, we see that in the last days God will not only clean us up, He will give us a fresh wardrobe.[37] The linen represents the righteous acts of His holy people.

Even our best efforts and most charitable deeds don't impress God if our motives are in the wrong place. Lots of folks do good deeds—they're called, "Uhh—good deed doers."[38] I'm not slighting them, but good deeds and righteous acts aren't the same thing. A "righteous act" originates in a heart that's devoted to God and is aligned to His will.

So, don't fill your calendar with deeds that will simply look good on your resume. A busy schedule may impress people, but God sees right through all that.

Turn your heart over to Him and then, your good deeds will be a reflection of His love for others. James 2:26 says, "Faith without works is dead" (KJV), and that is true. However, I would add, works without a faithful heart are dead too.

God really does care about cleanliness. If you don't believe me, read the book of Leviticus. There are over 100 references to God's ideas about what is clean and unclean. Like the bees, He's pretty focused on housecleaning. There is no neutral ground with God. Either it's trash or it's not. And if it's trash, it needs to go.

The expression "Cleanliness is next to godliness" is not in the Bible, but the Kingdom principle of cleanliness is. So when the junk begins to collect in your heart, take a lesson from the bees.

It may be time to take out the trash.

Are your deeds simply for show or do they come from a pure heart? What are some ways to keep your heart clean?

Search me, O God, and know my heart: try me, and know my thoughts: And see if there be any wicked way in me, and lead me in the way everlasting (Psalm 139:23-24).

Chapter 24 - What's That Smell?

So they set out and went from village to village, proclaiming the good news and healing people everywhere (Luke 9:6).

I love swarms if they're easy to reach safely, if they're large enough to survive, if they have a queen, and if they didn't come from one of my hives! Did I say I love swarms?

It's the first week in September, and Suki and I have caught a swarm of about 10,000 bees. The cluster settled in a tree near the hives and it wasn't too high which meant it would be easy to capture. We poured water on them so they wouldn't fly, and with a quick jerk of the branch we shook them into a cardboard box and transferred them to an empty hive in the apiary. We got the queen and most of the bees safely out of the tree and into the box, without any damage to the swarm or to us. Whew!

Yet, even though we're careful, we usually leave some bees behind. In this case, about fifty bees were still flying around the tree. They had lost the queen's scent and were confused. They didn't know where to go.

Back at the new hive, we gave the bees a small opening in the front so they could come and go, and then we watched to see if they would stay. You never know. Bees do seem to have a mind of their own, and bees are going to do what bees are going to do.

Soon, about thirty bees came out of the box and gathered at the front of the hive facing the entrance. As we continued watching, these girls stood on their tiptoes, lifted their tails in the air and began fanning their wings. Beekeepers have cleverly given this behavior a name. They call it "fanning."

Bees have an incredible sense of smell and these workers were fanning the queen's scent into the air. It's their way of telling all the bees in the area that this is where Momma is, and it's their new home. It's the bees' version of ringing the dinner bell that calls the kids in at dusk.

Think about it. A tiny honey bee, not much bigger than your little fingernail, can fan her tiny half-inch wings and send a scent into the air that other bees 50 feet away can smell! That's pretty impressive.

Soon the bees around the branch caught the scent of the queen, who was now in the box, and one by one they left the tree and moved in the direction of the hive. In less than 30 minutes, all the bees were once again reunited with their family. Meanwhile, the fanning bees, having completed their assignment, gradually began to go back inside. Within an hour all the bees had settled down and adopted the hive as home.

If only we could flap our wings and spread the fragrance of the Lord like that. Evangelism would be a breeze! Literally! Unfortunately, some of us don't know how to use our wings, while others don't think we're qualified to fan, and the rest of us don't want to leave the safety and comfort of our "home" to do the work.

Fanning isn't hard, but it does take focus. The bees positioned themselves at the entrance and adopted a posture to maximize their efforts. Likewise, the way we live places us in the right position too. Then all we have to do is take a stance (or be bold) and flap our wings to stir up the fragrance of the Lord in the lives of others.

Our first step is to pursue the Kingdom of God on our own, because we can't share something we don't have. The bees have been with the queen long enough that not only do they recognize her pheromone, but they also smell like her.

We each have to fill our own reservoirs. And as we do, we'll begin to take on the scent of the Kingdom. Once we smell like Jesus, we can re-present Him to others. That's how the Kingdom grows.

The next step is simple. Fan. All Christ-followers—even brand new believers—have the ability to fan. We don't have to be trained preachers. Our testimonies have the power of the

Holy Spirit behind them. As we glorify God, the Holy Spirit actually breathes life into our words.

Both the Greek and Hebrew names for the Holy Spirit mean breath or a gentle breeze. It's not by accident that in the Old Testament, God breathed life into Adam or that Jesus in the New Testament breathed the Holy Spirit into the disciples.

The Holy Spirit takes our humble words and breathes on them to fan into flame the heart cry of every person. We don't have to go to seminary for that, and we don't need any special training to tell our God stories.

Jesus sent out the disciples with an assignment to spread the good news. They obeyed and set out two by two—with almost no training. They spoke and God showed up with signs and miracles. He'll show up for us too. All He asks for is a willing heart.

There are lots of confused bees out there who are looking for a home. They're flying around aimlessly trying to find a place to land. And they need our help. A sweet smelling God story will draw them home. After all, the fragrance is on us. All we have to do is flap our wings.

What do you believe about your ability to share the gospel? Do you need to adjust your thinking in any way?

However, I consider my life worth nothing to me; my only aim is to finish the race and complete the task the Lord Jesus has given me— the task of testifying to the good news of God's grace (Acts 20:24).

Chapter 25 - Ready for the Harvest

"Your simple, daily acts of service may not seem like much in and of themselves, but when considered collectively, they become just like the one-twelfth teaspoon of honey contributed by a single bee to the hive." — M. Russell Ballard[39]

I love spring. After the long dark days of winter, when I see the tips of buttercups poking their green heads above the damp earth, I get excited. I know it won't be long before the bees begin poking their heads out of the hive, too.

The bees have been waiting for the warmth of spring, but they haven't been idle. They've been preparing for the harvest since January. Even though none of the bees in the hive are old enough to have experienced it, they know there's a "honey flow" ahead. And they're getting ready.

The day after the winter solstice (December 22), the queen slowly begins increasing the number of eggs she lays. In late February and early March, she begins to crank it up a notch. It takes three weeks for a worker bee to hatch, and it takes a lot of bees to make honey.

146

I monitor the buildup in each hive in this critical season making sure the queen is laying enough, but not too much. Too few eggs, and the hive won't have enough bees to gather nectar. Too many eggs and they could become overcrowded and swarm. So I take brood away from strong colonies and give it to the weaker ones to equalize the hives. The bees don't mind. If I've done my job well and if nothing else happens, all the hives will grow rapidly and the bees will make lots of honey for us both.

In Tennessee the harvest season is short. Our bees must gather almost all their nectar from mid-April through May. So when the "honey flow" begins, every forager bee shoots out of the hive like a rocket, making the most of every hour of sunlight.

Even working 16-hour-days and flying as fast as they can, each worker bee only produces about one-twelfth of a teaspoon of honey in her lifetime. That's not much in the grand scheme of things. Two teaspoons of honey in your tea are the life's work of 24 bees.

In a hive, there are no superstars, or bionic bees, who bring in a gallon of nectar. Every bee simply works on the task before her. There's an abundance of nectar to bring in; the hive only needs enough bees to collect it. The bees are a living example of the Kingdom principle of sowing and reaping.

Jesus said, "The harvest is plentiful, but the workers are few." He wasn't asking all of us to become great evangelists like Billy Graham. He was calling for every believer to do the task before them, like the bees do.

Sharing the gospel is more than leading someone through a prayer of repentance and salvation—it's cumulative. Like Nehemiah building the wall around Jerusalem.

Let me set the stage. The Jews had been exiled from Israel, and Jerusalem had fallen into ruin. Nehemiah, who worked for a foreign king, was given permission to go back to Jerusalem to rebuild the wall around the city.

The residents of the city had tried to rebuild the wall, but the task was too overwhelming. Any progress made was quickly nullified by Jerusalem's enemies.

After surveying the situation, Nehemiah noticed that many people were living in houses right by the wall's boundary, and he came up with a plan. He told everyone to only work on the section of the wall that was in front of them. With each individual and family simply doing their section of the wall, it was completed in 52 days.

We all began our journey as unbelievers, and some may still be on this rung of the ladder. Then we heard of a Man called Jesus. A number of us may be here. At some point in our lives, Jesus became a real Person to us, and we reached the next rung. Perhaps we repented of our sins, and asked Jesus into our hearts; we've reached the level of salvation. At this point, there are at least as many rungs on the ladder above us as there were below. No matter where we are on the ladder, we're not finished; we still have more climbing to do.

The process of sharing the gospel isn't about getting someone from the bottom rung to the top rung in one giant leap. The apostle Paul says it like this: (my paraphrase) One plants the seed and another waters, but it's really God who makes the seed grow.[40] While I love being the one to help someone enter the Kingdom of God, I'm also happy helping them up the next rung or two of the ladder. Sometimes I'm the one assisting someone as they climb, and sometimes someone else is pulling me up. Every step is important.

I used to watch the Billy Graham Crusades on television. Dr. Graham would step up to a podium in a coliseum and deliver a powerful message, and thousands would stream down the aisles to accept Jesus as their Lord and Savior. It was a life-changing step for those folks. However in the background still sitting in many of the seats, were the ones who brought those people to the stadium in the first place. God used Dr. Graham to reap the harvest, but those who planted and watered the seed (and drove their friends to the arena) also get to share in the reward.

We can't compare ourselves to Dr. Graham. He, like Paul, was chosen for a specific job. But like the Jews under Nehemiah's direction, and the bees who work to bring in all the nectar they can during the honey flow, we can do the thing God puts before us—help someone up the next rung of the ladder. Don't think what you have to offer is too small. God doesn't see it that way.

Your twelfth of a teaspoon is precisely what the doctor ordered.

What rung of the ladder are you on? Is there anyone you can help up the next step?

Don't you have a saying, "It's still four months until harvest?" I tell you, open your eyes and look at the fields! They are ripe for harvest (John 4:35).

Chapter 26 - Sweet Reward

"Not a single bee has ever sent you an invoice. And that is part of the problem because most of what comes to us from nature is free. And because it is not invoiced, because it is not priced, because it is not traded in markets, we tend to ignore it." — Pavan Sukhdev, United Nations report, The Economics of Ecosystems and Biodiversity[41].

Honey—that's the goal.

Year after year, every spring we add boxes to the hives to give the bees room to store that sweet reward. This year the girls have been working hard dehydrating and capping honey. And, once again, we're facing the long, hot, dry days of July.

It's harvest time—and it's hot! While the outside temperatures are hovering around 95 degrees, we're putting on our bee suits and getting ready to work in the bee yard—in the middle of the day, because that's when the foragers aren't home. I'm sweating even thinking about it! Any sane person would be inside sipping iced tea while the air conditioner purrs in the background. Did I mention it's July in Tennessee?

When we open a hive and start taking their honey, the bees aren't happy. They come boiling out the top pinging at your face! The smell of honey in the air not only stirs up the hive, it agitates other bees in the area, so we have to move quickly yet gently to get in and out before a robbing frenzy starts. One by one we visit each hive and remove any excess honey.

After we've contended with thousands of bees, we escape the bee yard with our loot, sweat dripping from our brows. Next, we begin the messy job of getting the honey out of the comb. We extract the honey in a room with temperatures above 85 degrees, so the honey will flow smoothly. Oh yes, and the room needs to be closed so the bees can't get in. If we open a window for air, the bees smell the honey and try to get in covering the screen so thickly they block the sun! It's a BEEclipse!

Once we're safely in the honey house where we extract the honey, we cut the wax capping off the comb, letting the wax and excess honey drip into the bottom of a tub. We'll collect and filter it later. Next, we put the uncapped frames into the extractor that spins the honey out of the comb.

The sweet syrup slides down the walls of the extractor to the gate at the bottom. It is filtered into a bucket, and filtered and filtered again. Then we let it sit, covered, in the warmth of the room for a few days so the air bubbles can rise to the top.

Of course, we've had a few tastes throughout the process. We call it quality control! It's a foretaste, if you will, of the day when our honey is set on the table and drizzled over a hot buttered biscuit. Talk about Heaven!

As yummy as it is, honey is more than bee sugar. It's the perfect food and contains everything to sustain life, including enzymes, vitamins, minerals, and water. In addition, it's the only food containing *pinocembrin*, an antioxidant associated with improved brain function. Scientists have discovered over 180 beneficial substances in honey—and they're still counting! It's the end product of tens of thousands of bees landing on millions of flowers and bringing back healthy bits of nature to mix with the nectar.

So whether you put that spoonful of honey on a biscuit or in your tea, you're exposing your body to little deposits of the environment where the hives were located. That's why local honey helps with allergies. When taken regularly over time, local honey has been known to lower blood pressure and cholesterol; it helps you sleep through the night; it's a probiotic and an antibiotic; it's an antiseptic and seals open wounds; and much more.[42]

I think honey is a great illustration of Heaven—there's more to it than meets the eye. Over the years we've diminished the riches of Heaven to clouds and wings and harps. But the Bible presents a different picture.

The New Jerusalem is a living city with gates of pearls, roads paved in gold and mansions. It's not a symbolic place, it has dimensions and measurements. And it's big. So big that it will require a new Earth to hold it. According to its proportions, if you were to place the New Jerusalem in the United States, it would cover almost all of the lower 48 states. It would be so tall that it could be seen from Africa.

In his Narnia Chronicles[43], C. S. Lewis suggests that even our most awe-inspiring surroundings on earth today are simply a shadow of the glories of Heaven.

I've been blessed to travel to some amazingly beautiful places on the earth: The Grand Canyon, USA—a mile-deep spider web of a hole filled with a full spectrum of color reflecting off hot rocks; the Amazon River, Peru—so broad it sometimes looks like a lake, lined with steep muddy banks and lush banana trees; the Karst Mountains, China—vertical spires defying anyone access, majestically pointing to the sky like victory fingers in a football stadium; the Sahara Desert, Mauritania, Africa—moving mountains of endless dry sand rippling like waves on the ocean; Waipio Valley, Big Island, Hawaii, USA—where the clear blue Pacific Ocean meets black sand and dense wet rainforest. Glacier Bay, Alaska—mile-high mountain ranges of ancient ice crashing to meet the sea.

The places I've mentioned are just a small sampling of the stunning scenery on the earth, yet all of this beauty is just a fallen version of what's in store for us on the New Earth. And let's not forget our new bodies. After His resurrection Jesus gave us a glimpse of what they will be like. He could walk through walls, eat food, appear and disappear at will and ascend into Heaven!

Somehow, I don't think we'll be bored.

God speaks of mansions and banquets, new bodies, a New Jerusalem, new Heavens and a New Earth—and then says, like the honey, there's more to it than we can imagine![44]

So, pull up a chair and pass the biscuits, please. My mouth is watering for some of that honey.

Do you believe the promises of God? What rewards have you been missing out on?

For no matter how many promises God has made, they are "Yes" in Christ. And so through him the "Amen" is spoken by us to the glory of God (2 Corinthians 1:20).

Chapter 27 - Bottling

Elisha replied to her, "How can I help you? Tell me, what do you have in your house?"

"Your servant has nothing there at all," she said, "except a small jar of olive oil."

Elisha said, "Go around and ask all your neighbors for empty jars.... Pour oil into all the jars, and as each is filled, put it to one side. . ."

When all the jars were full, she said to her son, "Bring me another one."

But he replied, "There is not a jar left." Then the oil stopped flowing (2 Kings 4:2-7).

Jars! Jars! Jars!

We have cases of jars stacked everywhere, because it's bottling time. The honey has been extracted and filtered. We've let the honey sit for a couple of days so the air bubbles will rise to the top. We also want to make sure the honey isn't too wet.

When the bees deposit honey in the comb it still has a lot of water in it (about 22%). So they start fanning to dry it out, just like they do when they fan the queen's pheromone (See Chapter 24). After the moisture level in the honey drops to about 19% the bees will cap it. Once it's sealed in wax, the honey can't absorb any water from the atmosphere so it will maintain a 19% water content, which is what the bees want.

Why is water content so important? Because if honey is too wet, it will ferment. Most people don't want fermented honey, unless they're making mead, which is another topic altogether.

When we remove frames of honey from the hive, not all the honeycomb is capped. Sometimes the bees haven't finished sealing every cell on the frame. The honey that's not capped probably isn't dry enough yet.

The bees naturally know when the honey's right, but we can't measure the water content by simply tasting it. We use an instrument called a refractometer. If the honey's too wet, we have to dry it out with heat lamps and fans. The dryer and thicker it is the better. We try to maintain an 18% water content in our honey. No one wants watered-down honey.

And you thought we just turned on a valve at the side of the hive and honey poured out!

With our honey at 18%, we're finally ready to begin bottling. Suki and I have a system. We sterilize the jars and lids. Suki hands me an empty jar. I place it under the five-gallon bucket valve and bit by bit I open the gate. The amber-gold liquid glides over the lip of the gate and oozes into the glass.

Once the liquid rises to the neck of the jar, I close the valve and with one last long thick drip the flow stops. I remove the jar and Suki wipes the rim in case any of the sticky stuff ended up on the outside. She screws on the lid, and we repeat the process. We fill and fill and fill until we either run out of honey or jars. It's an all-day process, but I don't mind. It's my favorite job.

Whether bees are filling cells with nectar or we're pouring honey into jars, I like to imagine that's how God fills us with His Holy Spirit, too. Yes, I know the Holy Spirit is sometimes described as a mighty wind, or a blazing fire, but He can also come over us like a blanket of honey, too—like liquid love.

Like my jars, the Holy Spirit fills us when we're empty, but He doesn't stop there. He doesn't want to simply screw on the lid and leave us neat and clean. He wants us to leak so He can keep on filling us. He fills and fills and fills. He's like the bee that daily brings us the nectar of Heaven.

In the Old Testament we see several examples of the Holy Spirit coming on people: Balaam, Sampson, Saul, Azariah, Zechariah, Ezekiel, Daniel to name a few. But He never stayed.

When Jesus was baptized, the Holy Spirit descended on Him like a dove, and He never left. He remained on Jesus throughout the rest of His earthly ministry. When Jesus ran low on the Holy Spirit's Presence, He would find time alone with His Father to get refilled.

After His death and resurrection, Jesus appeared to the disciples in the upper room. In John 20:22 He breathed on them and said, "Be filled with the Holy Spirit." He was imparting to

His disciples, and to us, the gift of the ongoing Presence of the Holy Spirit. So, unlike David in Psalm 51:11, we would never have to worry about the Holy Spirit leaving us.

Much later in Acts 1:4-5 Jesus gave them their commission saying, "Do not leave Jerusalem, but wait for the gift my Father promised, which you have heard me speak about. For John baptized with water, but in a few days you will be baptized with the Holy Spirit."[45]

The Holy Spirit was sent by Jesus to teach, comfort, inspire, counsel, and empower the disciples for ministry—and us too. Jesus knew we would need the filling and baptizing (Jesus' words, not mine) of the Holy Spirit to accomplish the tasks God gives us. Like the bees, Jesus doesn't want us to receive a watered-down impartation of His Holy Spirit either.

He puts His "super" on our "natural" to transform our Kingdom work from ordinary to supernatural. If Jesus needed the Holy Spirit and He thought the disciples needed the Holy Spirit, then I'm going to stand in that receiving line, too.

As Christ-followers let's cultivate a lifestyle of cooperating with the Holy Spirit. He's not an option like picking out what accessories you want on a car. He's as essential to Christ-followers as the car key is to start the engine. Without His Presence, we're ill-equipped for ministry and life.

Like the woman from the story in 2 Kings who kept filling the empty jars with an oil that never ran dry, Jesus wants to continue filling us with His Holy Spirit. Why not let God open the honey gate and fill you up?

I think it's His favorite thing to do.

Have you invited the Holy Spirit to empower your life? If not, why not ask Him now?

Peter replied, "Repent and be baptized, every one of you, in the name of Jesus Christ for the forgiveness of your sins. And you will receive the gift of the Holy Spirit" (Acts 2:38).

Chapter 28 - Labeling

"What's in a name?" — William Shakespeare, *Romeo and Juliet*

"Don't put a bug on your label." It was sage advice from the speaker at a Beekeeping Conference in Tennessee. Appearances are important and people are more inclined to pick up a jar of honey with a flower on it than a bee. After all, it's hard to enjoy a delicious spoonful of honey when you see a stinging insect staring back at you on the label.

Marketing any product is a challenge— whether it's a new software program, a clothing line, a novel idea, or honey. Even excellent products don't sell themselves. Marketing opens the doors to introduce your brand to the public. In advertising, catchy names, striking labels, distinctive logos, and eye-catching covers are carefully researched so one product will be chosen over others among the myriad of items on the shelf.

So when Suki and I started thinking about selling our honey, we took a serious look at what to put on our label. A friend of a relative of another friend designed a logo for us: a crown of honeycomb. We put it on a shiny black label with gold writing, added our brand name, a Scripture from Proverbs saying, "Eat honey, for it is good," and our label had the classy look we wanted.

Labels are critical when it comes to differentiating your honey from all the rest. And while creating your own unique look is fun, labels for honey are also regulated by the government. For instance, the word "honey" must be prominent and the net weight of your product in ounces and grams should be located on the front in easy-to-read numbers. The name and address of the manufacturer, packer, or distributor of a packaged food product are also required.[46]

Presentation is everything, so even if you recycle your jars, when you're packaging your honey, you never want to use an old label. We take great care to present our honey in clean jars with fresh new labels.

Labels. We all have them, don't we? They cover everything from our physical appearance to heart secrets. While some labels are positive, we tend to identify with negative words like: old, stupid, boring, fearful, dropout, insignificant, and angry.

For every negative word spoken over us, researchers say it takes at least five positive words to bring us back into balance. We're all prone to believe the damaging labels, which is why they stick so well.

Some labels are self-adhesive, and we put them on ourselves, but others have been applied by our parents, teachers or friends—some even come from the media: "Are you showing your age? Try our miracle-working ... " or "I lost 50 pounds with ... " It's the harmful tags that have the strongest glue. And, like gum on the bottom of your shoe, once they stick, they're hard to get off.

Bible teacher Beth Moore gives an illustration of labels like names on the back of a jacket. We try to hide them by wearing the jacket inside out, but the labels are still there. Others may not see them, but we do.

Carrying those labels around limits our lives. We're afraid to reach too high because those shameful labels might be exposed. So we stop short, saying, "Why bother? I'll never change." But, limited lives are not part of the Kingdom of God. They're lies from the enemy, who wants to hold us down. Jesus says, "I've come to give you life," and He does it *immeasurably more* than *all* we can ask or imagine. (Italics are mine.) That's a lot.

Last summer I was in New Mexico, and I saw a tee shirt that had a list on the back like this: "~~Alberk~~, ~~Albuk~~, ~~Allbukuer~~, ~~Albequerq~~, ~~Alburquerque~~, Albuquerque." I almost bought it for Suki because, unlike me, she's a good speller!

Crossed out names. Our jackets look like that. We hope the labels will fade with time, but when we look closely, we can still read between the lines.

God wants to erase those names permanently. He's not going to cross through our labels or slap others on top of the old ones, like travel stickers on a suitcase. He wants to peel them off, wash you clean, and give you a new set of names: Child of God, Righteous, New Creation, Blessed, Chosen, Royal Priesthood.[47]

Names are important to God. Names speak of our destiny, which is why God loves to give us new names. Just look through the Bible at some names He changed.

Abram became Abraham, which means Father of Many. Jacob, which means Liar, became Israel, which means May God Prevail or He Struggles with God. Simon became Peter, the Rock; Saul, a Hebrew name, became Paul, a Gentile name; and you ... God has a new name for you too because He's in the business of renaming us.

As a matter of fact, He promises to give us all a new name when Jesus returns. In Revelation 2:17 Jesus says, "To the one who is victorious I will give some of the hidden manna. I will also give that person a white stone with a new name written on it, known only to the one who receives it."

So take off that old jacket with the worn-out names, and throw it in the trash. It doesn't fit anymore. Why don't we step into the wardrobe and try on a new jacket, with a new name, that fits like a glove? I guarantee, it's a name to be proud of.

What's in a name?

Everything.

What labels have you been wearing? Is it time to exchange them for one of God's labels?

I will also write on them my new name (Revelation 3:12).

Chapter 29 - Distributing

Therefore go and make disciples of all nations, baptizing them in the name of the Father and of the Son and of the Holy Spirit, and teaching them to obey everything I have commanded you. And surely I am with you always, to the very end of the age (Matthew 28:19-20).

Whew! Finally, the honey is harvested, extracted, bottled, and labeled. Like a deflating balloon, the pressure gradually is released until all that's left is a limp noodle of rubber. We're limp too. We're tired, but satisfied.

After all the hard work over the year, I love to stop and admire the cumulative work of the bees: shelves lined with row upon row of sparkling honey-filled jars standing at attention like soldiers in their dress uniforms. It's a beautiful sight.

Nevertheless, if our honey sits on the shelf, those pristine jars will soon begin to gather dust. As good as the honey is, it's useless if I don't get it off the shelf and into the hands of my customers. Honey is meant to be eaten, not simply admired.

So now there's one last job to be done— distribute this sweet nectar to my friends, family, and customers. We fill orders, set aside jars, package the orders, update our records, handle money, reorder business cards, catch up with old friends, and make new ones. Kingdom business isn't a cookie-cutter industry. Like the many varieties of honey, it looks as different as each individual. But there is one common denominator. Like the honey, we have to get off the shelf.

In Matthew 28, Jesus told us to go into all the world to disciple the nations. Talk about leaping off the ledge!

But we don't have to sell everything we own and head off to the icy slopes of Greenland or the sweltering jungles of the Amazon to reach the nations. Not everyone is called to those remote places. The word *nations* (*ethnos* in Greek) has a broader meaning than just *countries*. It includes groups of people united by common descent, history, culture, or language, inhabiting a particular country.

The Greek word *ethnos* includes subgroups based on interests, needs and vocations, like: teenagers, seniors, businessmen, mothers, artists, and athletes. Each group has their own "language" and "tribal customs." Personally, I need a translator when I talk to a mechanic or a lawyer!

We all belong to an *ethnos* or two, and we already know the language. So don't pack your bags and head off to another country yet. There's probably at least one person in your tribe at home who needs to hear some good news.

Through enough study, I can understand some of the bees' behavior, but I'll never be able to communicate with them. I could flap my arms and make buzzing sounds all day long but clearly, I don't speak their language.

While bees can communicate with bees from other hives, scientists have yet to determine if they can communicate with other types of bees. I doubt a wasp would understand the waggle dance. It's that tribal language thing.

How many tribes do you belong to? I bet if you look around, there's someone in your *ethnos* who's searching for truth.

If we're harvested (become believers), then extracted (set apart from the world), bottled (filled with the Holy Spirit) and labeled (given a new name)—we can't allow ourselves to be content to remain on that dusty old ledge.

Isn't it time to take that jar off the shelf, unscrew the lid, and give someone a taste? It might be just what they're looking for.

What's your *ethnos*? Is there someone you can talk to who speaks your "language?"

And the gospel must first be preached to all nations (Mark 13:10)

Chapter 30 - Bee Yourself

"Honey Bee.
"Be Yourself" — Unknown

"How about 'Bee still and know that I am God'?" my friend suggested as I was walking out the door. *"Bee* still ... Get it?"

I smiled and nodded and tucked away the idea in my mental filing cabinet. After all, you never know when you'll need to open that drawer and pull out that file.

I can't tell you how many "bee" ideas were offered when I told folks I was writing a book about bees and the Kingdom of God.

I could also say: "To Bee or not to Bee. That is the question ..."

So when I found this quote, "Honey Bee Be Yourself," I knew it would be the perfect ending for the book. Notice I didn't say, *"bee* the perfect ending." There are so many opportunities to use a pun, but I'll try to restrain myself before you Bee-come bored.

Honey Bee.
Be yourself.
That's my point.

Have you ever seen a bee riding a motorcycle? How about a bee reading a book, watching TV, or writing a letter? Did you ever see a bee plant a tree or throw a ball? Of course not. Honey bees are busy being bees. They're not interested in being anything else.

As a matter of fact, if you look at any part of God's creation, you'll find it's content to be exactly who God created it to be. My dog, Simon, doesn't stare whimsically at a bird and howl because he wants to fly. He's not the least bit interested in driving a pick-up, although he does love a ride in the back seat of one. And he doesn't want to learn to climb, except when he sees a squirrel scampering through the yard and dashing for the nearest tree.

Out of all God's creation, we human beings are the only ones dissatisfied with who we are. Why is that?

May I propose an answer? Our identity is under attack. Our enemy, Satan, lost his position in Heaven because he wanted to be God, but he miscalculated. Now he takes out his revenge on God's children by attacking our understanding of who we are.

He began in the garden of Eden with Eve's temptation. He told her if she ate the fruit from the Tree of the Knowledge of Good and Evil, she would be like God. What she didn't understand was she was already like God because she was made in His image.

Throughout the Bible, Satan continued to attack mankind's identity. Here are a few examples: Moses, who was born a slave, raised as an Egyptian prince and ended up in the desert herding sheep; the Hebrew refugees in the desert, who still thought of themselves as slaves instead of God's chosen people; Saul, who was insecure as the King of Israel; David, who was anointed king, but hid in the desert for over ten years. The list runs through history all the way to Jesus.

At His baptism the Father had declared, "This is My Son..." and the Holy Spirit descended on Jesus. Then, He led Jesus into the desert. Satan met Jesus there and attacked His identity taunting; "If you are the son of God ..." It didn't work with Jesus because He knew the truth.

Satan's strategy does, however, work with us. He targets our identity with arrows dipped in jealousy and envy.

We compare ourselves to others, but we always come up short. It's always easy to look around and find someone who's doing great things and think, *Why can't I be like him? If I only had her talent, or his brains, or her looks, or ...* Let's stop trying to be someone else. No matter how wonderful they are, the world doesn't need two of them.

If you take away one nugget of truth from this book, let it be this: be the person God created you to be. You're one-of-a-kind; you're made in His image; and the world—needs—you.

God knew what He was doing when He created you. So, whether you're serious or carefree, emotional or stoic, artistic or structured, athletic or studious, — if you are all of these things or none of them—

Honey Bee.

Be yourself.

You're precious in God's eyes, and you have value. You may have stains and scars or bumps and bruises, but you haven't lost your worth. God loves you for who you are, not what you do. Let me say it again this way: God loves you— more than you know.

As a matter of fact, He thinks you're awesome! So, take a moment to "*Bee* still" and listen, with your heart. God has something wonderful to say to you.

Why don't you take one final moment and meditate on the following Scripture?

I am my beloved's and my beloved is mine (Song of Solomon 6:3).

One Last Note

I hope you've enjoyed walking down this path with me. While much of the hike has been uphill, it has been so much fun to stop and, like the bees, explore the flowers along the way. I must say, you've been great company— and incredibly good sports.

As I finish this book I realize I've learned even more about bees and the Wonderful One who made them. I hope you have too. While this trail is ending, I know there's another one around the bend waiting to be explored. I look forward to our next journey together—after all, there's always more ...

Thank you for spending time with me.

I hope to see you again.

Blessings,

M.J.

Glossary

The first time I went to a meeting of the local beekeepers' association, I was overwhelmed. I sat and listened as the speaker talked about managing honey bees. I knew he was speaking English, but the words didn't make sense to a novice like me. The more I listened, the more confused I became. Over time I learned the terminology and now I "speak the language" too.

I don't want you to be confused either. So here's a list of terms I'll be using.

Enjoy.

APIARY: It's not a family of apes. It's a place where bees are kept.

BROOD: It's not what you do when you deeply ponder something. It's the name for immature bees in the egg, larval or pupal (sealed) stages of development.

CELL: It's not a room where a prisoner is locked up. It's a small six-sided compartment of a honeycomb used to raise brood, store honey, and pollen.

COLONY: It's not a country under the political control of another country. It's an assembly of worker bees, drones, and a queen living together as one social unit.

COMB: It's not what you run through your hair. Also known as beeswax or honeycomb, it's the back-to-back arrangement of beeswax cells.

DRONE: It's not a remote-controlled aircraft. It's the male bee, whose function is the fertilization of a virgin queen bee.

EGGS: They're not what you eat for breakfast. The bee's life begins as an egg, which looks like a tiny grain of rice.

EXTRACTOR: It actually is a machine (either manual or motorized) used to extract something—in this case honey.

FOUNDATION: It's not the lowest load-bearing part of a building. It's a thin sheet of wax hung vertically in a hive. Worker bees add beeswax from glands on their bodies to draw the foundation into usable drawn comb.

FRAME: It's not the border of a picture. It's four pieces of wood assembled as a rectangle to hold beeswax comb.

GIRLS: They're not your girlfriends. Beekeepers often call their bees "girls" because over 95 percent of the bees in the hive are female.

HIVE: It's not a rash. It is a home for bees that is provided by man.

HONEY: It's not your sweetheart. It's the nectar gathered by bees from flowers and ripened into honey. It consists mainly of the two simple sugars glucose and fructose.

LARVA(E): It's not a tadpole. It's the second stage in immature brood life of bees between the egg and pupa stage.

PHEROMONE: It's not a made-up word. It's a chemical substance produced and released externally into the environment by an animal or insect, stimulating a response in others of its species.

PROPOLIS: It's not an energy drink. It's resins collected from trees or plants by the bees; used to close holes and cover surfaces of the hive.

QUEEN: It's not a reigning monarch. The queen is the mother of all bees in a hive. When newly emerged as an adult, she is called a virgin queen, while an egg-laying queen is called a mated or fertilized queen.

SMOKER: It's not a person who uses tobacco regularly. It is a ventilated pot in which a smoky fire is maintained with a bellows and is used to direct the smoke onto the bees.

SUPER: It's not an adjective meaning very good. It's any upper-story hive box placed over the brood chamber for the purpose of storing surplus honey.

SWARM: It's not a series of earthquakes near a volcano. It's a temporary cluster of bees that have left a hive with the queen. They will eventually move to a new home.

WORKER: It's not an employee. It's a female bee whose reproductive organs are only partially developed. Workers are responsible for all hive duties except egg laying.

End Notes

[1] *Excerpt from Here Comes Everybody: What's Next on the Web, Jan 8, 2009.*

[2] *www.gallup.com/poll/1891/snakes-top-list-americans-fears, 2001.*

[3] *John 15:13*

[4] *Hive boxes come in three sizes: deep boxes are 14 1/4 by 18 1/4 inches, 9 5/8 inches tall. Medium (or Illinois boxes) have the same dimensions except they're 6 5/8 high, and shallow boxes are 5 7/8 high.*

[5] *Bottom boards close off the bottom of the hive leaving a 1/2 inch opening along the front for bees to enter and exit.*

[6] *Matthew 16:18*

[7] *Atlas Obscura, Ranking the Pain of Stinging Insects, Lauren Young, June 2016.*

[8] *1 Peter 4:8*

[9] *Decline of Honey Bees a Global Phenomenon, says United Nations, Michael McCarthy, March 2011.*

[10] *Matthew 10:29*

[11] *"Just Do It" is an advertising slogan for Nike Corporation, Wieden+Kennedy agency, 1988-1998.*

[12] *Merck Manual of Diagnosis & Therapy, Merck & Company, 1899, 2011 (current printing).*

[13] *facebook.com/onelifemaps/posts — Quoted from Chuck Swindoll, So You Want to be Close to Christ, Word, 2005.*

[14] *"Mikey will eat it" was an advertising slogan for Life cereal, Quaker Oats, 1972-1984.*

[15] *1 John 3:2*

[16] *Matthew 6:33, Philippians 4:8-9*

[17] *Psalm 34:8*

[18] *2 Corinthians 6:18*

[19] *1 Corinthians 3:2, Hebrews 5:12*

[20] *Acts 4:13*

[21] *Exodus 3:1-10, 31:18, 34:29*

[22] *Bees may stay in their temporary location for a couple of hours up to a couple of days.*

[23] *Pew Research Center, April 2017.*

[24] *http://discovermagazine.com/1997/nov/quantumhoneybees1263.*

[25] *Bees don't store food in their bodies like we do. So to carry the largest load they can, they only eat enough honey to give them energy to fly from the hive to the flowers and back with little or no fuel left over. If they run out of gas, they will die in the field.*

[26] *2 Samuel: 6:14-15*

[27] *2 Samuel 6:22*

[28] *James 1:14-15, Romans 6:23*

[29] *Mayberry is the fictional southern town in North Carolina in the television series, The Andy Griffith Show, CBS, 1960-1968.*

[30] *Leviticus 25:1-5*

[31] *Isaiah 29:16, Jeremiah 18:6*

[32] *Matthew 9:22*

[33] *"Sounds of Silence" by Paul Simon, Columbia Studios, 1965.*

[34] *"To know God and to make Him known" is the mission statement of Youth With A Mission.*

[35] *Ephesians 2:10*

[36] *Psalm 18:2*

[37] *Revelation 19:6-8 & 14*

[38] *I couldn't resist using a quote from the Wizard of Oz, Metro-Goldwyn-Mayer,1939.*

[39] *American businessman and LDS church leader*

[40] *1 Corinthians 3:7-8*

[41] *July, 2010.*

[42] *The Honey Revolution by Dr. Ron Fessenden, MD, MPH, WorldClass Emprise, LLC, 2009.*

[43] *The Chronicles of Narnia, C. S. Lewis, 1958, Geoffrey Bles, U.K.; 1994, Harper Collins.*

[44] *Ephesians 3:20*

[45] *Acts 1:4-5*

[46] *Information provided by the National Honey Board, U. S. Department of Agriculture, Marketing Service.*

[47] *John 1:12, Romans 1:17, 2 Corinthians 5:17, Luke 11:28, 1 Peter 2:9*